Histor
Lovers

F. Lock

"THE BRIDAL MORN"

Frontispiece

Historic Lovers

W. L. George

BRACKEN BOOKS
LONDON

Historic Lovers

Previously published by Hutchinson & Co, London.

This edition published in 1994 by Bracken Books,
an imprint of Studio Editions Ltd, Princess House,
50 Eastcastle Street, London W1N 7AP, England

ISBN 1 85891 223 7
Printed and bound in Guernsey by the Guernsey press Co. Ltd.

CONTENTS

LIST OF ILLUSTRATIONS

CLEOPATRA

I. CLEOPATRA

A BID FOR EMPIRE

THE luck of history is exemplified by various characters. No doubt many women have loved as poetically as Mary Stuart, many women schemed as wisely as Cleopatra, and they are unknown. Their dust mingles with that of the ages, and the passing wind raises no wraith of them. But about the brow of a few women—and Cleopatra is one of these—history has twined a garland of thorns and of roses; over their heads it has cast a shimmering veil of romance, and given immortality without knowing it, without judgment or decision.

Why Cleopatra should live in our minds as a figure of magnificence and of passion, while the Queen of Sheba is naught save a biblical memory, while Clytemnestra is merely a bloody figure of legend, while the purple of Messalina has faded, is difficult to say. She was a lover, yes, but she loved a little too wisely for us to place her in the gallery of those women who loved to their destruction. It was not she that was destroyed, even though her life ended in the midst of love—they say from the bite of an asp; but the poison of the serpent which bit her breast ran to a heart that was calm. Calm certainly compared with the romantic tempest which blew in the breast of Mark Antony.

It may be unjust to say that Cleopatra loved neither

Cæsar nor Antony, just as it may be unjust to say of any modern girl that she does not love the man she marries. But the fact remains that Cleopatra purported to love just the two men who became practical rulers of her kingdom; she is exactly in the same position as the girl of to-day who, bred in a poor family, weds a millionaire. She may love the millionaire—millions make no man repulsive—but she is suspect, and Cleopatra likewise is suspect. Of the love of Antony we may be assured, just as much as we may deny that of Cæsar.

Presumably the fact that Cleopatra was queen of Egypt, queen of a land of immense ostentation and pageantry, made her romantic; also her death after defeat contributed; above all, the suicide of Mark Antony helped to make her immortal; the suicide of a lover is a woman's greatest advertisement. Thus for two thousand years the poets have remembered her, and Shakespeare alone might have made her immortal in half a dozen lines, which the writer quotes:

> Age cannot wither her, nor custom stale
> Her infinite variety; other women cloy
> The appetites they feed, but she makes hungry
> Where most she satisfies.

Such women there are, and such women survive, even though a realistic school sets itself up against the poets. For instance, Mr. Bernard Shaw says bluntly: "I do not feel bound to believe that Cleopatra was well educated. Her father, the illustrious flute-blower, was not at all a parent of the Oxford professor type, and Cleopatra was a chip of the old block." Still, Cleopatra will survive Mr. Bernard Shaw because mankind wants to believe in romantic love; and so with this doubt in our mind let us unfold the story of her short and tempestuous life.

Cleopatra was the last sovereign of the Ptolemaic dynasty, founded two and a half centuries before by one of Alexander the Great's generals. It will be recalled that Alexander came to Egypt as a conqueror and received divine honours, this being the method used by the Egyptians when they wished to placate a new master. Therefore Shakespeare has no right to call Cleopatra "sweet Egypt," for she was not an Egyptian. She was a Macedonian Greek, and in her genealogy we find no Africans. She came to the throne in circumstances of the most extreme difficulty. Her father, Ptolemy XIII, also known as Auletes, the flute-blower, left four children, Cleopatra, a son who was to be Ptolemy XIV, another son, and a younger daughter, Arsinoe. There was in Egypt no natural succession from father to son or father to daughter; the monarch might appoint whom he chose as his successor, and if a defeated candidate succeeded in establishing power by military force or by murder the Egyptians did not complain.

Auletes must have had this difficulty in mind, and he had good reason to, for the independence of Egypt was in his time, sixty years or so before the Christian era, a very doubtful matter. Technically it was a free kingdom, and it was not yet directly menaced by Rome. But Rome hung over the kingdom like a bird about to swoop; in fact, the predecessor of Auletes had named

Rome as his eventual successor. Auletes feared that during his life Rome would assert itself; therefore he went to Rome to bribe the senators, and to obtain from them recognition of his kingship. This was an easy matter, since almost every one of the Roman senators could be bought—since, in fact, a senator who took too small a bribe made himself unpopular.

Auletes was not exactly unsuccessful. Egypt being rich in gold and in jewels, he secured the support he wanted, and eight years after his journey to Rome was still king, but he was a shadow king. To bribe Rome he had been compelled to borrow money; his creditors sat in Egypt watching him, making sure of an eventual reward. There was a Roman army of occupation of entirely undefined status, rather akin to the British army of occupation which at this moment is to be found in Egypt. What was happening was that Rome maintained its rights without asserting them, and Auletes did not know when the heavy hand of Rome would descend upon his country.

That is, presumably, why, when he died in 51 B.C., he devised the following scheme to prevent civil war, and therefore to strengthen the Egyptian dynasty against Rome. Realising that Cleopatra and the child Ptolemy would each find partisans, and that one would enlist Rome, he decided to ignore the younger children and to identify the interests of his son and daughter by giving them the kingdom in common and by laying down that they should marry.

Marriages between brothers and sisters were not uncommon in that period, particularly for political reasons; besides, in Egypt they could revolt no man because the kings were divine, and therefore any royal act was a divine act. The marriage was therefore duly solemnised, though Ptolemy was several years younger than his sister, but there is no reason to believe that it was consummated; since Cleopatra in later years gave birth to children, it is likely that she would have given an heir as soon as possible to the uncertain dynasty.

Indeed, it is not until Cleopatra is twenty-one that historical events hurry upon her with the approach of Cæsar. Though the dead Auletes had procured the marriage of his son and daughter, and their joint royalty, to prevent civil war, yet civil war had to come, because joint royalty is impossible, because nowhere in the world has a queen succeeded in being queen when seated on a throne beside a king, because a consort will be tolerated, but not an equal. Both Cleopatra and Ptolemy had their flatterers, who realised that the triumph of one or the other would result in their advancement. A man of position at the court of Alexandria was never sure of his power or even of his life. If he obtained the favour of the king, he might lose that of the queen; if the king differed from the queen, he would naturally be tempted to make away with one of the queen's most important councillors.

It was therefore clear to the followers of Ptolemy that eventually Cleopatra would seek to assume sole power. The fact was equally clear to the followers of Cleopatra. Hence a conflict was inevitable, and it came over a court intrigue, as the result of which Cleopatra, cast down from power, and not at all assured by tradition that her life would be respected, fled to Syria, where she could find troops and allies.

Thus Ptolemy for a while reigned alone in Alexandria, one of the most magnificent cities of the East. One can imagine it as wholly Greek in civilisation, though Egypto-Roman in its government. A splendid picture of Alexandria, of its great harbour giving upon the Mediterranean, of the marble wharves, of the wall of the courtesans, is given in *Aphrodite*, by Pierre Louys. Its wealth was great because it was the most important commercial city on the southern Mediterranean coast. The nobles—all of whom were rich and mercantile—set in Alexandria a high standard of clothing and entertainment. There were philosophers—not equal to those of Greece—poets, musicians. Alexandria did not practise games as much as did Greece, but it was more Oriental, and thus partook of costly spectacles, of gilded processions, and of dancing rather than of field sports. Here was the wealth of Carthage without the skill of the Carthaginian or the bravery of Hannibal.

No doubt for a while young Ptolemy was happy, assured by his flatterers that he was the greatest monarch of the East, believing that he could make terms with Rome, and despising the sister who lay in Syria, a sister more ambitious, more intellectual, and more relentless than any woman whom Ptolemy could imagine. It was his lack of imagination and the folly of his councillors ruined Ptolemy. A little before these events, the tendency which had arisen in Rome to do away with the republic and to instal a monarchy produced, as it had done before, an able general. That was Pompey. It was then, and would be for some time, the Roman custom to exalt a successful general, to make him dictator, or, failing such exaltation, to allow him to make himself dictator. Nominally Rome was a republic governed by a senate; but, in fact, the senate was so venal and so cowardly that a legal or a practical dictator could easily establish himself.

Pompey, therefore, followed by legions which had fought under him and which loved him, recruiting allies by money and by force, set himself up against Rome. Cæsar, the great military rival of Pompey, was dispatched by the republic to overcome the rebel, whom he overcame at Pharsalia. Pompey could expect no mercy from Cæsar. He had before then seen many men tortured to death or mercifully slain; he had seen foreign kings walk behind the chariot of the conqueror in the Roman Triumph; and he was a proud man fearing ignominy. So, stripped of all power, his men scattered, he fled to Alexandria, where the councillors of Ptolemy made their mistake.

Instead of holding Pompey as a hostage, orientalised minds conceived that what would most please Cæsar was the death of his enemy. They did not at all understand the Roman frame of mind, its curious hardness, its respect for proper forms. They did not realise that Cæsar may have desired the death of Pompey, but would not tolerate his assassination. He would perhaps have executed Pompey after a trial which he would call fair, but only after a trial in the regular official Roman form. Also, Cæsar the Roman despised all non-Roman people. While the execution of Pompey at the hands of duly appointed Roman executioners would have been correct, his murder by debased half-Macedonian, half-African busybodies struck him as an unwarranted insult. Pompey might be a rebel, but he was a Roman, and the least of the Romans should be free from insult or destruction by anyone else.

Still, they murdered Pompey, and no doubt when Cæsar, in 48 B.C., arrived at Alexandria in pursuit of his enemy, they came to him satisfied with what they had done, and suggested reward. Cæsar dismissed them, established himself in the royal palace, showing Ptolemy no tolerance and little respect. Enquiring into the situation in Egypt, he decided to arbitrate between the young sovereigns.

And here comes the first romantic adventure of Cleopatra, an adventure where daring mixes with a certain comedy. She decided to come to Cæsar and to obtain his support against Ptolemy. She was twenty-one, and charming; in her mind may have formed a plan to secure Cæsar as a man before she secured him as a political ally. She may have expected this, for she had been admired, and indeed Cnaeus had wished to marry her. But she could not have believed herself to be beautiful. The reputation of Cleopatra as a beauty has been bequeathed to us by history, and yet the few sculptured representations of her features do not justify any claim to the apple of Paris. From the British Museum bust we see that Cleopatra has a very short, almost round head, a brow higher than the Greek standard of beauty requires, eyes that can be described only as ordinary, a pleasant enough mouth, the upper-lip somewhat thick and therefore significant, and a nose which we would to-day call disagreeable. It is thick, distinctly curved, and coarse about the nostrils. It is not a Greek face, it has none of the noble relationship between the planes of the cheeks and those of the jaw which have immortalised the Greek type.

If Cleopatra triumphed over men, it was not by beauty. The one claim to attention may have been a certain whiteness of skin. According to Lucan she was white enough to cause reference to the fact in a country where nearly all women were dark. It is just possible that the eyes were blue, that the hair was golden, since such a type existed, and still exists, in the Balkan States. But Cæsar had known many women with blue eyes and golden hair. Cleopatra's influence must have come from herself, from some gaiety, some spirited reserve of her nature. We have traces of this in her relationship with Antony, and we find it in her introduction to Cæsar, which provides us with another inference, that she was small.

Cleopatra had followers in Syria, but she realised that a formal march upon Alexandria would result in a battle which must be uncertain, in her death if she were captured, and possibly in Roman brutality. She must not waste time over battles, and she must not allow Cæsar to pronounce too easily in favour of her brother. So Cleopatra disguises herself, as many a woman did in the Middle Ages, and by night enters Alexandria, accompanied by her faithful servant, Apollodorus. In her daring she arrives at the gates of the palace. She is queen, she might demand admission, but her brother is in power, and the quick thrust of a sword might end her pretensions before she could put them forward.

So the little queen—for she must be a little queen or Apollodorus could not achieve the feat—is placed in a sack. The sack is hoisted upon the shoulders of her faithful henchman, who marches past the sentries into the palace, passes among the servants. None is disturbed by this obvious slave who carries a burden to the kitchens, but Apollodorus knows the ways of the palace, and in a few moments enters Cæsar's room, deposits the burden at the feet of the Roman. The sack is undone, and out of its mouth appears the laughing head of the little queen, who looks up at the great general. One may imagine that Cæsar laughed, not knowing perhaps that here was Cleopatra, taking it perhaps that this was an amusing companion, sent him by his host Ptolemy, to beguile the tedium of a soldier who had left his wife at home.

How the conversation proceeded between Cæsar and Cleopatra is naturally unknown. Whether the queen flung herself upon her knees as a suppliant, or whether she dealt with the Roman as an equal, is beyond a guess. It is not likely that she supplicated him, for her spirit was too high. Nor is it likely that she sought to tempt him, because she was preoccupied with imperial designs, not with the impulse to amorous adventure. It is conceivable that she stated her case to Cæsar, that she showed him that she had a right to the throne, which would not move him at all; that she was a woman of brains, of which he would take note; that she might supply a valuable ally to Rome—to that he would listen. Finally, she would allow him to perceive that she had wit, vivacity, charm, and that she was twenty-one. Cæsar was fifty-four, and to him this argument might appeal.

The relationship which was set up between Cæsar and Cleopatra cannot therefore be entirely ascribed to the Egyptian queen. In the case of Antony it is certain that Cleopatra played upon the feelings of a rough soldier, but in Cæsar she had to deal with the coldest, most cynical man whom Rome could then produce. Cæsar had lived a long life of dissipation; he respected neither his own marriage nor that of other men; his adventures among the wives of leading Romans were notorious, and only his power had saved him from assassination. But he was also a patrician, a man of culture, who has left us in the shape of his commentaries a work that is recognised as a classic; we know from his behaviour when taken by pirates that he had sardonic wit, for he refused to be ransomed at the price the pirates stated, saying that he was worth much more, and insisting upon doubling the ransom. Finally, he was the greatest soldier the world knew, and carried about his head the massed laurel-leaves of the conquests of Gaul and of Britannia. Here was an experienced man, a magnificent figure, and, though not young, a man seasoned by camps, a good horseman, expert in use of arms: was he not the natural hero of a young woman's dream?

The present writer does not believe that Cleopatra approached Cæsar like a siren. Cæsar would not have become the victim of her wiles; for forty years he had been a lover, and he knew all the wiles of all women; he would have been amused rather than conquered by coquetry, capriciousness, or any of the scanty tricks of the feminine repertory. If anyone was the victim it was not Cæsar, but Cleopatra.

Still, whatever may have been the origin of the relationship, it was established. Cæsar decided to stay in Alexandria, to keep order there, the Roman peace, to arbitrate between the two sovereigns. Since Cleopatra now stood to him in a relationship so tender, this amounted to saying that he proposed to establish her upon the throne. Here we may hasten history by saying that the subjection of Alexandria was not easy, for the population was hostile to Cleopatra because the Roman favoured her. For some time there is war between the Romans and the Egyptians, which ends suddenly. Ptolemy's fleet is sunk, and he is drowned. Alexandria, devoid of a sovereign, now lies at the feet of Cæsar. With Cleopatra at his side, he enters as a conqueror into the great Oriental city.

The magnificence of the Queen of Sheba must have surrounded the ceremony. We may imagine Cleopatra in ceremonial Egyptian costume, for she then discarded her ordinary Greek vestments. Her hair would be braided with pearls, and strings of pearls, each one as large as a pea, would hang upon her breast. Upon her fingers, wrists, ankles, toes even, uncut emeralds and rubies would glow. She would be carried in a litter by the side of the triumphant Cæsar, while slaves, crowding about them, struck rhythmic musical instruments and held over their heads a canopy of purple studded with gold to avert the Egyptian sun. And there would be much feasting in the palace. The night would be lit with torches, inflamed by wine, and no doubt ensanguined by the execution of captives, the ordinary compliments to the Roman triumph and an example to which Cleopatra, barbarous as the Romans, hotly fierce where they were coldly savage, would easily accept. So we have a vision of the moon casting its silver radiance upon white-flagged courts, where flow together rivulets of blood and wine.

It is impossible to say whether the marriage of Cleopatra and Cæsar originated from the mind of a girl intoxicated with a brilliant man, or from the calculations of an ambitious general. There were advantages on both sides : Cleopatra by wedding the most powerful man in Rome—and therefore the most powerful man in the world—was achieving the object which all through her life animated her, the protection of her crown and her dynasty ; Cæsar, on the other hand, was acquiring, without effort and without risk, Egypt and all that was in the sphere of influence of Egypt ; also, he obtained a precious jumping-off ground for an expedition against Persia, against India, for a march into the unknown world—therefore a world where should soar the eagles of Rome. He who had brought Gaul and Britain into the Roman realm might now gain the credit of conquering the East.

Marriage was a simple matter, because Cleopatra, according to the Egyptian conception, was divine. Just as Alexander had received divine honours, so were they given to Cæsar. As her husband he was the incarnation of the god Amon, and it was Amon who, through Cæsar, fathered her child, Cæsarion. Professor Weigall, in his *Life and Times of Cleopatra*, the most important book that has been published on the subject, considers that this display of hypocrisy, this divinisation, must have worked upon the semi-epileptic mind of Cæsar, and encouraged in him the dream of monarchy which was already there. But for Cleopatra he might have been content with the dictatorship of Rome. After Cleopatra he wanted Empire, and the woman by his side, as ambitious as he, must have seen in this dream of the imperial purple, not only the protection of her dynasty, but its exaltation. She, the slave at Cæsar's feet, might enslave him. Queen of an uncertain kingdom, she might make her child emperor of Rome, emperor of the world.

According to Mr. H. G. Wells, in *The Outline of History*, Cæsar was an elderly sensualist, who dallied with young Cleopatra. Certainly at his age the young queen must have been infinitely attractive, but it should be said in his defence that he did not hesitate to leave Cleopatra, after the birth of their child, to complete his victory over the followers of the dead Pompey, whom he routed at Thapsus. Only after this did he send for Cleopatra to witness his triumph at Rome. He was dictator for the third time, and Cleopatra attended the triumph, not as a captive, tramping in chains in the dust behind the chariot of Cæsar, but as his bride, as a jewel as precious as Egypt. And though Cæsar probably had no faith whatever in the gods, since no Roman gentleman believed in such nonsense, he paid Cleopatra a pretty compliment: since she had declared him to be the incarnation of Amon, he declared her divine by placing her statue in the shrine of Venus.

But here were the Ides of March, and Rome was not

yet ready for empire, not having suffered enough from strife, being willing to throw itself into the arms of a strong man. Not all men loved the dictator. He had rivals—Antony, Octavian, especially Octavian, who was to be Augustus; these two were capable of desiring empire. Also there were democrats—men such as Brutus, Cassius, and others—who loved the republic, and loved themselves a little. They had tolerated a dictator, but here stood before them an Oriental monarch, wedded to a savage queen, a man who thought himself a god. It was too much for them. Such a man would soon attempt to make himself a monarch; he must be destroyed. Thus the plot, thus the support acquired by money, by promise of power, of enough senators. Thus Cæsar, suddenly surrounded by the conspirators, and thus Brutus, son of Servilia, whose lover Cæsar had been—Brutus perhaps the son of Cæsar—delivering the last thrust of the knife which made Cæsar exclaim: "And thou, Brutus!"

Thus the downfall of Cleopatra. Now she was in a hostile city, relict of a hated man. It must have crossed her mind that Rome had no scruples, that here was the moment for Rome to slay her, slay her child, destroy all of her dynasty except the forgotten Arsinoe, and make Egypt into a province. Still, Cleopatra was preserved, not by mercy, but by rivalry. The Romans did not trouble themselves with complicated questions, such as the rights of Cæsarion, heir to Egypt, heir to Cæsar, and perhaps in a sense heir to Rome, since Rome might have been his father's heritage. After the death of Cæsar they took to the strife of faction, and Cleopatra was able to return to Egypt.

Was she safe ? She was, for a little time, while the chaos of Rome produced the triumvirate, a government by three men—Mark Antony, Octavian, and Lepidus. She was at rest for five years, during which some sort of organisation was given to Rome, during which the murderers of Cæsar were defeated and punished at Philippi—by Mark Antony, the avenging Mark Antony, the noble servant of the shade of Cæsar. Absurd indeed, this comedy of history, for the noble Antony warred for Cæsar to inherit from Cæsar, because the triumvirate could not maintain itself. There was no room in the world for Mark Antony and Octavian. Perhaps Antony knew this, and perhaps he sought to add to the credit he had gained at Philippi by bringing into the empire the kingdom of Egypt. So, in 41 B.C., we find him at Tarsus, requesting the Egyptian queen to come to his camp and discuss politics.

Whether Cleopatra hesitated, whether she resented this invitation, is difficult to say, but already there must have formed in her mind the idea that she had triumphed over Cæsar and thus protected herself, that she might triumph over Antony and protect herself again. She could not trust Antony as a politician ; he was quite capable of having her assassinated—or at least so she assumed, not then knowing the Roman. On the other hand, it was vital that she should acquire the support of Antony, because the support of one member of the triumvirate would weaken the others. Therefore she made terms with Antony, and ranged

J. L. Gérôme

CLEOPATRA AND CÆSAR

Octavian against her. Therefore she concentrated hatred between these two and averted it from her own head. Octavian was the nephew of Cæsar. Cæsarion was the child of Cæsar. Obviously Octavian would be against her child, so Antony must be for it.

And she was clever. She knew that the Roman was barbarous, heavy, and dull-minded. She decided to impress him, just as African explorers have impressed ferocious negro tribes by means of a gramophone. At Tarsus she refused to dine with him, and made him come aboard her galley, where she had concentrated the wealth of Egypt, a perfection of cooking fit for Lucullus, music, costly raiment, and much wine, with which she plied Antony. And she staggered him by taking from her ear her greatest pearl, dissolving it in vinegar, and drinking it before the eyes of the Roman, distended with cupidity and with surprise.

That year Antony marched to Alexandria, allied himself with Cleopatra, and became her husband. Did Cleopatra love Antony? Who is to say, when again advantage goes with happy matrimony? If only Cleopatra just once could have loved a mere captain of her guard, we should be sure—but she was so exclusively addicted to imperial figures. She may have loved him, for Antony was a younger man than Cæsar, and as superior to him physically as he was mentally inferior. He was then forty-two, and a man of enormous proportions, unusually developed in the muscles of the neck and chest. The photograph of the bust which lies before the present writer shows a low, animal brow, masses of curly hair, a great hard chin, full lips, high cheek-bones, and deep-set eyes. There is in the face brutality and simplicity. Antony is more akin to the Goth, who four hundred years later would come to sweep Rome away, than to the intellectual Roman. Set by the side of Cæsar he is the bulldog, while Cæsar is the greyhound.

Like most very large men, he was amiable until he was crossed ; he enjoyed his strength, liked field sports, ate and drank abundantly, and enjoyed the society of boon companions, with whom no doubt he sang songs and exchanged coarse jokes. He had acquaintance with women of refinement, such as Fulvia, who was married to him, but he had probably never before met a woman such as Cleopatra. Fulvia was a good woman ; Cleopatra was different. He had known slaves, and Cleopatra was his slave, except—well, was she his slave ? One can imagine how this must have puzzled the heavy man. He had not met nimble-minded women ; he knew how to handle a Roman matron, the most uneducated and stupid type that Rome had produced, and he knew how to deal with a coarse courtesan. But Cleopatra, who had ideas on policy, while he understood only battle, was bound to triumph over him.

It is presumable that Cleopatra loved Cæsar better than Antony, because at twenty-one a woman loves a man of fifty-four more easily than in later years is she attracted to a natural mate. But of Antony's passion for Cleopatra there is no doubt at all. She responded ideally to his mood, because she was gay, high-spirited, because both liked ceremony and magnificence. Plutarch relates many tales of their life together, of their rivalry, of their habit of disguising themselves and at night coursing about Alexandria, knocking on doors and running away—just as Mary Stuart collected revellers about her to stir the dark echoes of the Puritan Canongate: high-spirited queens vary but little.

However, Antony could not long stay in Alexandria to indulge in his new passion, for the world was in turmoil. His party at Rome, headed by his wife, whom he had forgotten in the arms of Cleopatra, was struggling with Octavian, and was soon overcome, having to flee Italy, while Octavian installed himself in power. The brave but stupid soldier must have been lectured by Cleopatra, who realised that against Octavian she must set up an empire of which Antony would be master. Besides, the East itself was in turmoil, now that the name of Cæsar no longer spread terror. Syria, that lay so near the borders of Egypt, was in revolt, and the Parthians, those nomads of the north-east, whose cavalry could prevail even against Rome, were threatening the borders of the realm where Cleopatra strove to maintain the Ptolemies.

In fact, it is probable that Cleopatra decided to give the fire its share, and not to deal peacefully with Octavian. Whether her influence can be traced to it or not, a reconciliation between Antony and Octavian was somehow achieved. Fulvia was dead, and served as a convenient scapegoat. Octavian was good enough to believe that Antony was not responsible for the faction fight in Italy, and that the dead Fulvia was to blame. Also, Octavian probably realised that his time had not yet come, that he needed to organise and to arm before he could overthrow Antony, making himself master of the whole empire. Thus the empire was divided between Octavian, who received the whole of the west, including Italy and Rome, Antony, who was given the east, and the insignificant third member of the triumvirate, Lepidus, who received northern Africa. So far so good for Cleopatra, but here came a fatal fact: the treaty between the rivals was solemnised by the marriage at Rome of Antony and Octavia, sister of the new Cæsar.

Here was disaster indeed for Cleopatra. She had made an enemy of Octavian, and Antony was playing her false. No question of bigamy arose, since it would have been sufficient for Antony to hand her a bill of divorcement to make him free to marry Octavia. Cleopatra could have reconquered him, but she was in Alexandria, and he in Rome, where her eyes could not play upon him. Indeed, he might forget her; he might make terms with Octavian. He might conspire with Octavian, and Egypt would serve as the joint booty for their plunder. So for three years she stayed alone upon her uncertain throne, no doubt already conscious of impending doom, for she experimented upon criminals the effects of poisons, gathering information that might be useful in time of disaster.

But time was with her, and Antony did not love Octavia, another Roman matron, ill-educated, and fit to weary any man. Master of the East, he must return to the East, and thus must meet Cleopatra. They met at Antioch, and it would be good if we had notes of this interview, for Cleopatra must have called Antony faithless, must have vowed that she would deal with him only as queen with dictator. Antony must have explained, have pleaded policy, insisted, said he could not help it, that he disliked Octavia, that he loved only Cleopatra, that it had all been a misunderstanding. The big man must have been dull enough to have argued and protested to an angry woman. And the more he protested the more he apologised, the more completely Cleopatra asserted herself over him. Perhaps, at length, Antony took the only possible course, snatched up Cleopatra in his arms, declaring the past to be an ugly dream, and begging her to take him back, never to release him. And Cleopatra graciously extended her hand to raise to her tottering throne the master of the East. Octavia was forgotten, and now Cleopatra was legally married to Antony, while Cæsarion, the child of Cæsar, was recognised as heir to the whole of the eastern empire.

Thus Cleopatra had triumphed: her dynasty did not yet inherit Rome, but it inherited her own Egypt and much, much more than she had dreamt of in the early days.

They were happy. Cleopatra felt secure, and Antony drank and amused himself. We have a hint of their relationship in the following story. Antony being simple and very vain, liked, when he fished in the harbour of Alexandria, to catch many fish and to collect the court about him, so that they might applaud his skill. Cleopatra discovered this foible, and one day with the court came to the wharf to watch the prowess of Antony. Almost at once Antony uttered a sound of pleasure, and began to haul in his line, crying out that he had caught a fish. But, much to his mortification and to the delight of Cleopatra, the fish when landed proved to be a salt herring, which one of the queen's divers had for a joke attached to the line of Antony.

Such women are loved, and such a story brings imperial Antony near to us, makes him attractive; it causes us to see Cleopatra as an ordinary sportive woman behind the imperial figure. But Antony could not indefinitely rest in his new Capua, for the Parthians were pressing upon the borders of the eastern empire. Indeed, they defeated him, so that he had to return to Egypt to collect troops and supplies; only by overcoming the enemy at the gate could he hope for security within. Meanwhile, minor complications were forming. Antony's wife, Octavia, accompanied by a Roman bodyguard, was advancing towards him to beg him to return to Rome, and to forsake Cleopatra. Antony would not meet Octavia. Perhaps he was afraid of her tongue. He had been lashed at Antioch by Cleopatra, and, like a whipped dog, brought back to Alexandria, where he was chained into matrimony.

Antony was not the man to confront two wives, and so took the easiest way, war, for he feared Octavia much more than the Parthians. And the war was successful, so that, his pride restored by victory, he returned to Alexandria to celebrate his triumph. This was the first triumph that any Roman general had celebrated outside Rome. That deed marks the turning-point in the career of Antony, and perhaps marks his doom. Now that he has triumphed in Alexandria, he has declared himself to be an eastern monarch. He no longer depends upon Rome, and therefore he is an enemy of Rome. There was in that period no room for two Romes, just as there was no room for two men. Antony in his madness feasted in Alexandria, forgetting that there he could not find power, but only pleasure, forgetting Rome, the central ganglion of the world. Traitor to the Roman tradition, he pressed gifts upon Cleopatra, giving her Syria, Arabia, giving her Roman land. Her son Cæsarion he named " King of Kings."

Meanwhile the madness of empire was invading Cleopatra, who at that time used an oath which ran as follows : " As surely as I shall one day administer justice on the Capitol." It was mad, for the East cannot conquer the West, and one hears in the voice of Cleopatra the cackling of the geese which once saved the Capitol of Rome. War broke out for several reasons : Cæsarion was more definitely the heir of the Roman Empire than Octavian, since he was the son of the dictator, not merely a nephew ; also Octavian was a tyrant in Italy, and a democratic movement still existed, ready to take the field against him. In fact, the reasons were simpler : Octavian hated Antony, and perhaps Octavian feared Cleopatra.

Indeed, Cleopatra held the aging Antony enthralled as she had never held Cæsar. Though Antony's Roman legions and his senators feared and detested her, envying her power over Antony, she made him divorce Octavia, so as to reign alone over his heart and mind. Perhaps Antony was aware of this, perhaps he grew afraid of the world movement he had instigated, for soon after this he collected his legions and made them one of the magnificent, sonorous speeches of which he was an adept, where he incited them against Octavian, and vowed to restore the Roman republic in its pristine beauty—that is to say, in its brutality to slaves, its crucifixions, its floggings, its official corruption, and its complete licence in married life.

And now the end. The East was set against the West, and the East could not prevail. We find Antony setting up his camp at Actium, on the coast of the Ionian Sea, opposite Italy, at the heart of Octavian's realm. He is strong, but he is disunited. He holds a Roman army and an Egyptian fleet; thus he suffers divided councils, for the Roman generals know only the land, so would war only upon the land, would send Cleopatra back to Alexandria, taking issue with Octavian's army upon Italian soil. But Cleopatra, using the nimbleness of her mind upon his dullness, soothing him with love, intoxicating him with wine, begs him with her navy to face that of Octavian, so that the sea may be clear, so that there may be no long campaign in Italy, but a naval expedition and a landing within a few miles of Rome. Perhaps Cleopatra feared a victory upon the land as much as a defeat upon the sea, for a land victory would be the victory of the Roman generals, who hated her. If they triumphed, might they not triumph over Antony? Might they not reduce her once again to widowhood, to the occupation of an uncertain throne?

She prevailed. On the second of September, 31 B.C., the two navies met off Actium, to engage in the fight that was to destroy the East and make Octavian master of the world. The forces of Antony were defeated, and here comes a tragic fact; seeing that the day was lost, that Octavian triumphed, Cleopatra collected what remained of her ships and drew away from the battle. Perhaps she loved Antony, but one doubts whether a woman who loved would have chosen to flee, even to procure her safety, and whether she would not have preferred to die by her lover's side. Antony loved Cleopatra, and she did not love Antony. She loved only her dynasty and her throne. The flight of Cleopatra marks the rout of the East, for Antony was now so dependent upon his eastern queen that he too fled and followed her.

Disaster! Antony—beaten, disgraced, misanthropic, despised by his few followers because he has failed, deprived of power by Cleopatra because she can rely upon him no more—now flits about the coast of Egypt, already a shadow, though he lives, while Cleopatra, realising that the vengeance of Octavian will not stop, strives to build up the East for the conflict that must come. She was crazy with fear. She was growing middle-aged, and could not hope to have much power over men, so, while Antony in Alexandria tried to drown his sorrow in wine, she sent Cæsarion, now seventeen, to find allies in Hindustan. But Octavian marched into Syria.

It was over. For one moment Cleopatra was in safety, when Octavian offered to leave her Egypt providing that Antony died, but she could not trust Octavian: she loved Antony no more, but still he was a great soldier, and she could not throw away his life on the word of the cold, the self-seeking, the heartless Octavian. So the Roman drum threw its sounds into the south, as the Roman armies marched through Syria, as they reached Sinai. Louder and louder these drums—drums of fate—until Alexandria was surrounded, until Antony, gallant and foolish to the end, seeking no terms with his enemy, led his forces in the last struggle and was defeated. The Romans were pressing, the streets of Alexandria were filled with the riotery of the terrified people, and there came to him a rumour that Cleopatra had killed herself. It was too much. He had laid upon that charming brow too great a store of emotion ; he might lose an empire and conquer another, but he could not forget Cleopatra. Surrounded by the few friends who clove to him, he allowed himself to fall upon his sword.

But Cleopatra was not dead yet. She received the dying Antony in her arms, and perhaps soothed his last moments by a smile. Yet she was not thinking of him, perhaps hoping that even now, in her forties, her charm might prevail ; perhaps a third Cæsar would fall at her feet. But Octavian was cool. He cared not for women. Cleopatra saw that all was lost, and threatened to make an end of herself. Octavian warned her that her children should die, that her dynasty should be blotted out. Cleopatra fought to the end, begging of Octavian neither life nor throne, but only recognition for Cæsarion as his heir to the Roman purple.

Octavian said neither yes nor no, and she was in anguish. He kept his counsel, and yet it came to Cleopatra that not only death awaited her, but infinite shame : she was to be sent to Rome, she was to be a captive, and, with chains upon her wrists, to tramp the dust behind the chariot of the victorious Cæsar, as he triumphed in Rome. Then indeed she must hurry death, and cheat it by taking with her own hands what the executioner would give her. We do not know how she died, perhaps by poison, perhaps—and it seems more fitting, because more barbaric—by the bite of an asp.

Romantic is the scene—a room in the palace, floored in white marble. From the window can be seen the smoke of battle, which soils the sky of blue and gold. Upon a couch, while Charmian, the waiting maid, weeps, lies the woman who has ruled over two Cæsars, whom a third Cæsar overthrows. A white hand takes from a slave a basket of roses, which she bends to breathe. She holds them to her breast, and within the flowers lies coiled the serpent that carries doom. She holds it close, the scented deliverance. The fangs pierce the white skin, and Cleopatra lies upon the couch, waiting for death. She dreams of a long life, of Cæsar's face, sharp as a knife, of his wit, and her laughter; of Antony, burly Antony that lies so still, who led his life with her, accompanied by the trumpet's blare. Dear Antony, he loved her. Perhaps she loved him a little too.

Her eyes begin to blur, and her hands and feet are cold. This is death, this the quiet ending to so much desire. Perhaps she thinks again of Antony. Perhaps even she thinks of Octavian—fool that she was not to enslave him! She will not die; she will go to Octavian. He shall know her beauty. He shall love her; he shall enthrone her. She will be queen of the East, queen of the world. . . .

But her frozen tongue can speak no word. "She is dead," says Charmian, as she raises the serpent to her own breast.

BIBLIOGRAPHY

The Life and Times of Cleopatra, Queen of Egypt, by Arthur Weigall.

Cleopatra, her Life and Reign, by Désiré de Bernath.

Cæsar and Cleopatra, by Bernard Shaw.

Antony and Cleopatra, by Shakespeare.

Cleopatra, by John Lord.

GEORGE SAND

II. GEORGE SAND

A WOMAN IN BREECHES

One fact must be remembered in judging George Sand: she was in no respect what may be called a well-brought-up young lady. Though her grandmother strove to bring up the child as a Victorian figure, George Sand early refused to convert herself into the trim, cool, and timid young person which was the ideal of the eighteen-thirties and forties. Let us waste a little space on saying what was this ideal. It is expressed in *Renee Mauperin* by the brothers de Goncourt, through the mouth of the heroine:

> "When we are dancing, do you suppose that we may talk to our partners? 'Yes, no,' 'no, yes'—that is all we may say. We have to keep to those monosyllables the whole time. That is being well behaved! There is one of the charms of our existence! And it's all like that in everything. 'Proper' is another word for simpleton. And then to be condemned to chatter with one's own sex. When one has the misfortune to run away from them to the society of men—I have been well scolded by mamma for that! One more thing which is not 'proper,' and that is reading. It is only two years since I have been allowed to read the stories published in the newspapers. Then I am made to skip

all the crimes which are reported; they are not 'proper' reading for me! It is the same with the accomplishments that we are allowed to have; they must not go beyond a certain point. Beyond a duet and a lead pencil, everything is regarded as affected and exaggerated. For instance, I paint in oils, and by so doing I make my family miserable. If they had their way, I should be only painting roses in water-colours."

George Sand, who was to become a great, though not a very great, writer, was ill-fitted by heredity for such a career. The origins of George Sand were extraordinary. In the dim eighteenth century King Frederick Augustus of Poland grafted its first recorded misalliance upon George Sand's family tree, a misalliance which was also an irregularity: the courtesan Aurora von Konigsmark bore him Maurice de Saxe, the famous general who in 1745 defeated the English at Fontency. Maurice de Saxe allied himself, irregularly again, with a lady whom courtesy called an actress, and thus through a second misalliance was born Aurore de Saxe. This lady married a M. Dupin, and here comes the first legal marriage. But the son of Aurore Dupin discovered a favourite in Sophie, who was nothing but a camp follower in Napoleon's army. Here occurred the third misalliance, but it was followed by a marriage; of this marriage was born Aurore Dupin, who was ultimately to reach fame as George Sand.

So much tempestuous blood, so much carelessness of convention, must operate to excuse in the mind of the reader a career which was certainly scandalous, but which would not have been scandalous if George Sand had been a man. Her misfortune was that she was born in skirts when she should have been born in breeches. Educated by her grandmother, she succeeded in reading Rousseau, Voltaire, all that was forbidden to young ladies; in her girlhood she acquired the habit of smoking cigars, and at last the breeches were cut out of black velvet and worn, to the great scandal of the neighbourhood. In other words, she was eccentric.

If Mdme. Dupin had lived, the career of George Sand might have been a little different; she might have married better, and thus she might not have been exasperated into alliances which were often foolish. Unfortunately the grandmother died when George Sand was seventeen, leaving her in the painful position of having a guardian for her fortune, while all the instincts of an affectionate nature drew her towards her mother, a woman common, uneducated, and silly, but whom George Sand loved because she was her mother, just as later she loved her own children because she was their mother. Simplicity pervaded George Sand's nature.

The consequence of this unpleasant situation, a struggle between two guardians and a call to two different social levels, was that George Sand fled into marriage as other women flee into nunneries. She married a M. Dudevant, a good-looking man and perhaps a well-meaning man, but the most unfortunate husband imaginable for a woman of brains and temperament. His only interests he found in cattle and in the fields ; he drank ; his wife irritated him, and he did not hesitate to beat her. Finally, he was unfaithful to her. Naturally the high-spirited girl, little over twenty-one, would not tolerate what so many women tolerated a hundred years ago ; she aspired to express herself in speech and in writing ; she needed intellectual stimulus—and she was asked to live with a man who ordered her to pull off his muddy boots after a day's shooting.

Thus, suddenly, George Sand leaves her husband at their country house at Nohant, forsakes her children, taking, however, great pains to provide for their well-being ; she flees to Paris, where almost at once we find her living with Jules Sandeau. It should be recalled that in the eighteen-twenties France granted no divorces. However unfaithful Dudevant might be George Sand could obtain no redress. Under such conditions it was impossible for her to regularise her situation, and so, like George Eliot, she deliberately set aside the marriage bond. Thus begins her long love odyssey, where always she seeks that which she cannot find because nature has cast her in the wrong sex.

It would be wearisome to analyse one by one the amorous adventures of George Sand. Several are ridiculous, and one is contemptible ; only two of her liaisons, with Alfred de Musset and with Chopin, deserve the notice of history, because only these involve a man of merit equal to, or greater than, hers.

It is enough to say that Jules Sandeau was a clever young man of twenty, who wrote with her and helped her to write, with whom, when she was twenty-seven, she conducted a typical household of artists; he was clever, but he was not more, and so suddenly the link was broken, when he proved unfaithful to George Sand with—irony!—a young washerwoman. Yet Jules Sandeau has left us an attractive picture of George Sand:

"She affected a kind of petulant brusquerie, the result of a secret uneasiness, and an ardour that ran to waste. She had almost a man's familiarity of address, so that it was easy to be intimate with her, but her haughty chastity and her instinctively aristocratic air mingled with her 'abandon' certain suggestions, as it were, of a virgin and of a duchess, contrasting strangely with her disdain for the proprieties and her ignorance of the world. All the evidence revealed in her a richly endowed nature, stirring impatiently beneath the weight of a wealth not yet called into activity. Life—palpitating life—seemed to move among the curls of her beautiful black hair; and there burnt as it were a hidden fire beneath her delicate and transparent skin. The purity of her brow indicated that the storms of passion had not yet broken upon that noble head; but the expression of her eyes, burning, yet weak and tired, spoke of terrible interior struggles, ceaseless but unavowed."

This passage conveys her charm, and it was a charm rather than a beauty. The picture of George Sand by Charpentier shows us a woman with large features, a heavy mouth and a heavy jaw, but the dark eyes, under beautifully drawn eyebrows, are full of fire, full of nobility. Indeed George Sand was noble, but she was as immensely foolish as people of talent know how to be. For instance, she met Prosper Merimee, a hard intellectual, somewhat superior to her in the art of writing. He did not love her, but he was flattered by the emotion of the clever and handsome young woman. He allowed her to throw herself at his head, and he allowed her to adorn his brow—for a week. Perhaps George Sand was as much to blame, since here we detect the masculine side of her character: she could not have stayed allied to Merimee because he was too masterful, too much of a man.

Here the present writer takes issue with most of the literature dealing with George Sand, which is abundant. Nearly all the commentators of George Sand have spoken of her motherliness. Because she was attracted by men of weak physique and feeble health, it has been said that she was motherly. She was so, and her correspondence contains many tender letters to her children, letters to friends showing that she was preoccupied with their welfare, but motherliness was in George Sand a form of the protective spirit which is common in men as well as in women. She loved de Musset and Chopin as she loved her children, and that because she could protect them, lead them, dominate them, because her attitude to men amounted to the attitude commonly found, not in women, but in men. That is why she could not be happy with Merimee, any more than later she could be happy with Michel, the well-known barrister. She could not tolerate a masculine man, because she herself was more masculine than he.

Other names occur in the adventures of George Sand, people like Mallefille and Leroux, but this side of her life is still bounded by de Musset and especially by Chopin. For the present chapter would be unjustified if it were merely a scandalous chronicle; what matters in her relations with Chopin and de Musset is that they make us understand her better, and therefore enable us to understand her work.

Alfred Musset has descended in the history of French poetry as a delicate rather than as an impassioned singer. He was good-looking and effeminate, but he had good taste, belonged to an aristocratic family, and so it is likely that he was conquered mentally rather than physically. Indeed, at that time George Sand had written several novels which illustrated a peculiar and entirely novel talent. Her books, such as *Indiana*, *Lelia*, *Elle et Lui*—all these books express the French eighteen-thirties and the great romantic movement. This movement must be understood if we are to compass George Sand. It was a reaction from the formality of the eighteenth century, when manner and morals were carefully arranged and codified, when love was expressed by a blush, and faith by an inclination of the head.

The artifice of the eighteenth century, an artifice of powdered courts, created in the breast of Rousseau a sort of rage. He hated the powder, the theatre, the scent, the fraud of society. He proclaimed the return to nature, the natural innocence of mankind, the beauty of primitive people. After Rousseau came Bernardin de Saint-Pierre with his *Paul et Virginie*, with its ideally pure heroine, who drowns at sea rather than remove her clothes before a sailor. There comes Chateaubriand with *Atala*, and *Les Natchez*. Here the movement is more pronounced, for, not content with the return to nature, Chateaubriand idealises the noble savage.

A strange wave of imbecility passed over French literature: the Red Indian—who was unclean, treacherous, cruel—appeared as a noble figure, an example for corrupt European society. A fantastic modernist excitement passed through literature; noble attitudes became the rule, and later Victor Hugo with his great brass band heralded in the procession of kings, gods, heroic hunchbacks and misunderstood convicts. Lions proved merciful; courtesans were purified by true love. In other words the period was the victim of what is called sensibility, and what was actually sentimentality. That period needed the rough brooms of Flaubert and de Maupassant. The George Sand period had called a spade an agricultural implement; the Flaubert period called it merely a spade; and the Zola period was to call it a damned spade. George Sand lived in a period when no such indecent word as spade was supposed to be used in literature.

That infuriated her. She wanted to live, and therefore was determined that other people should make no mistake about it. Hence, perhaps, the adventures—since many of us believe that one cannot "live" unless one lives a little scandalously. George Sand was proclaiming in this way "woman's rights." Her novels are full of protests against the marriage relation; she demands for woman not political rights, but emotional rights, the power to love whom she chooses, and how she chooses. In other words, she is a pioneer.

" GEORGE SAND "

She follows Mary Wollstonecraft, and she does something to break way for the suffragists who are then unborn.

All this had its effect upon de Musset. His weakness found some assurance in the masculine mentality of George Sand, but almost at once love arose between them, on the side of de Musset rather light and self-satisfied, on the side of George Sand generous (George Sand always gave herself for ever, but soon began to shorten eternity). She inflamed de Musset into verses so beautiful that one translates them with hesitation. Still, here he addresses George Sand:

Again thou hast invaded my starry nights,
Angel with azure eyes and eyelids shrouded,
Love, my supreme good, a good which I had lost!
I thought thee for three years to curse and yet to vanquish,
And thou with weeping eyes and with thy tender smile,
Thou hast returned, my bedside thou art haunting,
While two words of thine have made me king of worlds.
Lay thy hand on my breast and feel how deep the wound;
Deepen that wound, my angel, and may my heart so break!
Never did lover love, for his mistress a dying
Drink a draught more divine in eyes that were so black,
And on a nobler brow ne'er did man lay kisses.

The reader must not conclude that Alfred de Musset failed to remember the eyes of his beloved. The azure eyes are those of the angel of love, and the dark eyes those of George Sand. The contrast is perhaps slightly unkind. Thus the relationship between de Musset and George Sand developed; they lived the Bohemian life of the nineteenth century, meeting chiefly writers, critics, and such. They went for a honeymoon at Fontainebleau, and the months passed until at last there came to George Sand a deeply masculine instinct: she wanted to take her beloved away, into some distant country where they would be alone, and where she might slowly devour him. Suddenly she asked de Musset to go with her to Italy. He goes, but a slight absurdity enters the romance: Mdme. de Musset and Alfred's brother Paul are consulted, argue with George Sand, argue with Alfred, fearing more for his health than for his morals.

The power of George Sand is here witnessed, for Mdme. de Musset in a letter to a friend says: "She employed all the reserves of eloquence of which she was a past mistress to induce me to entrust my son to her, assuring me that she would love him like a mother, and would take greater care of him than I should myself. And so—what can I say? The siren snatched a consent from me." Here, indeed, is a tribute to the extraordinary charm of George Sand. What mother would have consented to such a relationship unless her heart were moved and her eyes bemused?

The journey to Italy, which took place when George Sand was thirty, was wholly wretched. George Sand lived in a constant state of mental activity—writing, writing, spilling ink upon table and floor, setting down ideas between kisses. Meanwhile de Musset showed himself indolent, spent his time at cafés, dancing, and amusing himself with Italian acquaintances of the female sex. In other words, we have the picture of a hard-working man taking to Italy a flighty, clever girl

—but the man was the woman, and the woman was the man. Naturally, de Musset, being of weak physique, could not endure this life. He became ill, and now enters one of George Sand's absurd adventures, that with the Italian doctor, Pagello, from whom develops an emotional tragedy.

De Musset is ill, according to some having *delirium tremens*, according to others typhoid fever, and perhaps merely Italian malaria. Pagello prescribes for the sick poet, while George Sand grows madly irritated with the feebleness of her lover. She turns to Pagello, because he is well and strong. Exasperated by the sick-room, she falls into the arms of the young Italian. Pagello is commonplace, a small-town doctor. He is overwhelmed and amazed by the woman, more radiant more intelligent than any he has met before. Forgetting the old love, forgetting her responsibility, George Sand cries out in exultation:

"Yes, I can still love. Those who said that I could not lied. None but God can say to me, 'You shall never love again.' . . . To be happy for a year and then to die!—this is all I ask from God and from you. Good-night, dearest Pietro."

Then, in her wildness, she forsakes de Musset; she drags Pagello in her train—a Roman conqueror with a captive behind his chariot—drags him to France; then forgets him, discards him, giving herself once more to a fury of creation of novels, two or three of which she could write in a year.

And so we come to Chopin. Here was again a man of delicate health and high-strung temperament. Moreover, he had recently been crossed in love, and was naturally liable to attraction. In this case, as usual, George Sand was the aggressor, and it is said that, after listening while he played one of his nocturnes, she leapt to her feet, flung her arms round his neck, embraced him, and said, with justice, that he was one of the heaven-born. Thereupon Chopin, who was vain, fell more and more under her sway. He was in some senses akin to Alfred de Musset, except that where de Musset recalled a foolish and flighty girl, Chopin suggested a foolish, cranky old maid.

They became lovers, and as soon as this was achieved George Sand felt rising within her the impulse she had known before. She must have her beloved to herself to eat him at leisure, and, just as she had taken de Musset to Italy, she took Chopin to the Balearic Islands, Spanish islands in the Mediterranean. She was happy for a short time, but, as in Italy so did little by little unhappiness come. The place was adorable, a land covered with palm-trees, where orange- and olive-trees bloomed in the open ; but Chopin was ill, consumption working within his breast, and so expecting George Sand to attend to him, instead of playing the lover. Meanwhile she worked day by day as she always did, while Chopin complained of the primitive island where facilities for washing had not been thought of, where forks and spoons were scarce (in 1838 the Balearic Isles were as primitive as are to-day the backwoods of Peru).

Finally, for by this time George Sand had obtained a judicial separation from her miserly and drunken husband, Chopin accompanied George Sand to Nohant. And here too she suffered from the querulous invalid.

He disliked the food, he hated the weather; for both he blamed George Sand. He loved her, in spite of himself, and for eight years he spent his summers at Nohant, as a friend rather than as a lover. But George Sand exhausted him with her excitement, with her enthusiasms for people, for books, for political causes; even her enthusiasm for his music worried him after a while, and gradually, one hardly knows how, the parting came. No doubt she decided to dismiss Chopin as she had dismissed Mallefille and Leroux, for George Sand was man enough to get rid of people when they had ceased to please. Liszt describes in a few brutal sentences her attitude to Chopin:

"Mdme. Sand caught her butterfly, and tamed it in her box by giving it grass and flowers—this was the love period. Then she stuck her pin into it when it struggled—this was the congé, and it always came from her. Afterwards she vivisected it, stuffed it, and added it to her collection of heroes for novels."

This is unjust; it takes no account of the broad generosity of George Sand's nature; it leaves out the fact that, though she was not a technically chaste woman, she always looked upon an alliance as a marriage: thus she was absolutely faithful. In her long life there is not one story of intrigue; she keeps herself entirely unto the man whom she has chosen. She gives herself freely, entrusts herself wholly, and withdraws herself honestly. She behaved like an honourable man, and this should entitle her to some respect.

No doubt Chopin was partly to blame for the parting. He was—one cannot call it anything else—crotchety.

He quarrelled with George Sand because she detected in his music imitative harmony—in other words, what we to-day call programme music; he quarrelled with Liszt, charging him with playing Chopin as Chopin did not write; because he was a dreamer he resented being aroused; he was difficult. Also he was vain, and when he went to London rejoiced intensely in the popularity which met him there. He was presented to Queen Victoria by the Duchess of Sutherland; he gave a recital at the house of Lord Falmouth; he was a lion. And thus, lonely and still young, he died, far from George Sand, who would have loved him to the end, who would for him have released those deep springs of motherly feeling which she expended upon her children.

Here let us end this chapter upon closer indications of George Sand's mind and of her position in the world, saying only that after Chopin, apart from a rather foolish and cheap adventure, there is nothing in her life except work and maternity. When Chopin left her she had reached the age of forty-nine; she was middle-aged, and perhaps her fiery spirits were at rest, unless they sublimated themselves in work, and in her political interests.

A perusal of George Sand's letters, which make up three large volumes, reveals a woman whom one cannot help liking because she displays together warmth of heart and intellectual brilliance. For instance, when she is twenty-three she writes to her mother a pleasant, chatty letter, ending with the following graceful phrase: "Good-bye, my dear mamma; excuse my being a little out of temper with you, and pray let me see that you remember the daughter whom you possess in Berry, and who loves you more than you think." The domestic note is indeed strong in George Sand. If she had had a kind husband who allowed her to write, to love her children and to love him, she might have made no scandalous history. Many letters to her son Maurice have been preserved. She writes about his health and recommends changes of stockings; in 1831 she tells him that she is buying him a National Guard uniform, and describes the uniform of the Hussars. She even tells him to give her love to his repulsive father; generosity could not go further than that. Again, she writes to the boy: "I am very satisfied with you, my dear child; you did not cry much while I was there. Tell me what you did after I was gone. Did you like your little dinner-service? Do you think it pretty?" In the same year she writes to ask whether Maurice has received a toy she sent him, and tells him a story of a mouse of which she made a pet.

One does not want to exaggerate what may seem perfunctory, but, in fact, the warmth of her heart appears all the time when she writes to Maurice or to Solange, her daughter, for she never says a word against their father. She lives away because she must, not because she wishes to.

There is, however, another side in the George Sand letters, namely the correspondence with politicians and with artists. That with the politicians is particularly interesting, for George Sand, born in 1804, the year of the crowning of Napoleon, was all her life a democrat, indeed a revolutionary. She made friends with the great Mazzini, to whom, as well as Garibaldi,

Italy owed freedom; she was a great friend of Barbes, one of the Communists imprisoned by the French republic of 1848. In that type of correspondence we recognise a broad mind which could hardly settle down in the country with a yokel husband:

"I see nothing but ignorance and weakness among the majority of the dwellers on this globe of ours. The struggle, I am aware, has begun in earnest, we shall perish in it, that is my consolation. After us, progress will follow its course. I have doubts neither in God nor in man; but I find it impossible not to proclaim the bitterness of the stream of anguish and suffering which carries us."

Again, she writes in 1848: "What can those do who have devoted their lives to the ideal of paternal equality, who have ardently loved mankind, and who worship in Christ the symbol of the people redeemed and saved? In short, what can socialists do when an ideal deserts the bosoms of men, when humanity despairs of itself, when the people desert their cause?"

She was incensed by the triumph in 1848 of the French bourgeois republic over the socialist people. She was in the mood of a follower of Lenin when he saw established over Russia the democracy of Kerensky. She was an extremist, and found that other extremists lacked her idealism. It angered her to see France seek a king or a bourgeois republic. She summed up her period in a fine phrase: "There is not one man who feels in himself what he is and what he must be." She is in other words an idealist, always generous, for she writes to Mazzini: "Those who tell me that our object is to reach personally some more favourable and smiling lands are regular children who believe themselves certain to live a whole century." This thought has been better put by the poet who said: "Other little children will bring my boats ashore." But the generosity is there, as it always is in impetuous, unhappy, greedy, capricious and tender George Sand.

One discovers her generosity of mind in other ways. For instance, in 1853 she writes to Silvestre to recommend to his support the work of the painter Delacroix; in 1857 she writes to the Empress Eugénie to beg the support of the sovereign for a grandson of Marie Dorval, the actress, and she approaches the Empress as a mother. What pleases in this letter is the thought of the effort which George Sand, republican—socialist indeed—must have made to write to one whom she looked upon as a tyrant. But she could not help the boy, and the Empress could; that was enough for the kind heart of George Sand.

However, the reader should not conclude that George Sand was a sentimentalist. Her masculine mind was tender, but she could fight, and summed up life by saying: "Peace at any price is a delusion, and that which is bought by cowardice is but a ruthless annihilation that does not even afford the poor advantage of a lingering death." It is, therefore, not remarkable that such a woman should have been recognised by men and women of eminence. Apart from her lovers, two of whom are famous, apart from Mazzini and from Barbes, we find in her acquaintance the names of most of those who achieved a greatness between 1840 and 1860. A woman who could become friendly with Arago, Balzac, Berlioz, Delacroix, Alexandre Dumas, Flaubert, the brothers de Goncourt, Heine, Liszt, Mazzini was no small personality. Many of these attended her funeral, where were also present Renan and Prince Napoleon, while Victor Hugo wrote her oration.

Her correspondence with Flaubert is perhaps the most interesting of all: in the first place because no question of love arose between them, George Sand being many years older than Flaubert; in the second place because Flaubert embodies the most austere talent that ever gave itself to the novel.

In her letters to Flaubert we find many acute phrases, no longer intimate or political, but literary phrases, those of a woman who is a conscious and conscientious literary artist. At the age of sixty-two she half-excuses her life when she writes to Flaubert: "Our excesses of work, as our excesses of pleasure, kill us certainly, and the more we are great natures the more we pass beyond bounds and extend the limits of our powers." Flaubert evidently respects her judgment, and with her discusses his plans: it is a pretty compliment. She strives to express herself more fully; she tells him that the ideal of justice she cannot see apart from the ideal of love; she conceives a society where all human beings shall help one another as the bees help the bees, and the ants the ants. George Sand is never selfish; hardly ever vain. She is as a torch that burns, careless of its own extinction, provided that it may burn.

If George Sand, instead of being born in 1804, had been born in 1870, she would have been a greater writer. Instead of taking her first intellectual food from Rousseau and his sexual romanticism, from Chateaubriand and his ecstatic Byzantine Christianity, she would have fed her brain from Flaubert, Renan, de Maupassant, Huxley, Darwin; she would have stood by the side of Zola as one of the leaders of the naturalistic school. She would have been a greater writer, but she would not have been a greater woman. She would have been as fallible, and perhaps she would not have been as generous. We may sum up the quality of gallantry which makes George Sand a gentle memory by quoting from her last letter, the letter which she wrote to Dr. Favre two days before she took to her bed, never to rise again:

> "Thanks, dear friend, for your kind letter! I will follow all your prescriptions. To the report I sent you yesterday, I will now add my reply to the questions you put to-day. The general state is not worse, and, in spite of my age (almost seventy-two) I do not feel the symptoms of senility.
>
> ". . . But a portion of life's functions being almost entirely suppressed, I wonder where I am going to, and whether I must not be prepared to go off suddenly some fine morning! I should prefer to know now, rather than have the surprise. I am not one of those who are afraid at the prospect of submitting to a great and general law, and rebel against the conclusion of universal life; but I will, in order to get cured, do all that is prescribed to me, and should my fits leave me a day of rest, I will come to Paris, so that you may help me to lengthen my task; for I feel I am still useful to my family."

Mdme. de Pompadour died gracefully; she detained the priest and said: "One moment, M. l'Abbé, we shall leave together." George Sand died generously, thinking of her kindred and of mankind. She too knew how to die.

BIBLIOGRAPHY

Readers interested in this character will find fuller information in the following works:

The George Sand-Gustave Flaubert Letters, trans. by Aimée L. McKenzie.

The Letters of George Sand, trans. and edited by Raphæl Ledos de Beaufort (3 vols.).

The Life and Letters of Chopin, by Noritz Karasowski, trans. by E. Hill (2 vols.).

George Sand and her Lovers, by Francis Gribble.

Madame Sand, a Biographical Comedy, by P. Moeller.

Une Histoire d'Amour, by Marieton.

HELEN OF TROY

III. HELEN OF TROY

THE CURSE OF APHRODITE

ONLY those who can compass the magic of Greek verse will entirely compass the magic of the story of Helen and of Paris, the disaster of Troy, and the sombre tale of gods warring with and among men. Not the formal and rigid lines of Pope, not even the charming fantasy woven by Andrew Lang about the brow of Helen, can translate the story which Homer tells and the immortality which he afforded to Helen.

And yet, when we read any of these translations, even when we peruse *The Legend of Fair Helen*, as told by Oswald with a thoroughness that clips the wings of Apollo, still beauty hangs about the tale. Told even in a version for schools, it is a vision of something light and yet profound, which has been ground down, soiled, spoilt; it is nothing but a rag of an immortal banner, and yet it is beautiful. It is something that men cannot destroy. In the story of Helen we have the whole fantasy which Greece has bequeathed to us and which the world will never quite forgo. Here we find the touching Greek conception of the gods, so much more intimate than ours; the conception of a fate in which we believe no more; of these tablets of bronze where the lives of men are written before they begin to lead them; of the great wars, the smoke of battle raised by the dust of the chariots, of mighty blows inflicted by irresistible swords upon armour that cannot be pierced.

It happens in a realm distant from our imagination, a realm roaring with battle, flowered with blooms which the imagination cannot raise, haunted by songs sweet as the voice of the Rhine maidens.

Whether the story of the flight of Helen with her lover and the story of the fall of Troy before the avenging Greeks are true or not is a question not easily decided. It is practically certain that Troy existed on the coast of what is to-day Asia Minor. The ruins of the great city, possibly three thousand years old, are well defined. They lie according to a noble plan. Their faint vestiges, fainter even than those of Carthage, allow us to see that Troy did exist, that Troy did fall. And it is also probable that Troy did not fall before an eastern horde. Lying by the shore of the Ægean Sea, it was the natural goal of the Greek invader. It fell before the Greeks. Whether the origin of the quarrel was the flight of Helen is, on the other hand, rather doubtful.

Assuming that the date of the Trojan War was the year 1000 B.C., it is difficult to believe that the Greeks would have for nine years prepared a war which lasted ten years merely because some local chieftain—a Menelaos who would not be known to history but for the story of Helen—lost his wife to a favoured Trojan lover. Mahaffy gives of the Greeks in the Homeric period a picture which does not at all concord with the idea of an enterprise so chivalric. Such a war might have been conducted by Don Quixote. It is possible that a group of knights in the Middle Ages might have placed themselves at the head of an army because one of their number had been despoiled of his wife; but the excited, lyrical point of view which lay at the back of chivalry and of the crusades did not exist in Greece. It never existed there. Neither the pastoral Greeks, three thousand years ago, nor the cynical, imperial Greeks, two thousand years ago, would have gone to war for anything so trifling as the most beautiful woman in the world. For conquest, yes, or for plunder, but not for a woman.

The early Greeks lived in a state of semi-barbarity, in low houses devoid of proper heating arrangements, devoid of ventilation, none too clean. Their weapons were elementary, their cooking-vessels suggestive of the age of bronze. They were a simple, rather rough people; without being cruel, they were brutal; unwanted children they exposed upon a height so that they might die of cold or be slain by the eagles; their lives appear to have been fairly pure, rather akin to that of the German tribes which Tacitus describes; they were hospitable, which is natural in a country where all travellers depend upon hospitality, and afford it so that in turn they may enjoy it.

In a civilisation so primitive woman had not a position of importance, except that she was the vehicle of the race, that she provided children, who were necessary to the husband for the perpetuation of his name and for the provision of devotees who would sacrifice to his manes and pacify angry deities. She was practically bought from her father, or given by him as a reward for a political alliance, or for prowess in the field. She had to submit to the polygamous male, to the presence in her household of favoured slaves; she might be queen of the harem, but she was not more.

Is it conceivable that enterprises so great should have been directed by a woman's eyes? It is impossible. If we assume the existence of Troy, we may say that certain Greek settlements must have for many years envied the power and the prosperity of Troy. There may have been Trojan wars, but we know nothing of those which antedated by many years the war in the course of which Troy fell. It is possible that the Greeks did not prevail in these early encounters. It is much more likely that the various chiefs of the Greek tribes were disunited: the tragedy of Greece was always its lack of unity. Though the Greeks could coalesce occasionally, as they did against the Persians, in the main the whole story of Greece is one of rivalry, where Corinth hates Athens, where Athens hates Patros, where Sparta despises all.

Since in a much more civilised period the tendency of the Greek tribes was towards hostility, we may assume that three thousand years ago, when common interest was still not recognised, hostility must have been still greater. But the feeling against Troy may slowly have brought the tribes to agree against a common enemy. If then, when Greek unity was temporarily achieved, a sanguinary personal insult was put upon Menelaos, one of the confederate chiefs, it is conceivable that here was a rallying signal, and that the Greeks went to war for plunder, telling themselves —as men do to-day, and as men no doubt always will—that they went to war in pursuit of a noble ideal, the redressing of a wrong done to one of their number.

However, we may leave this theory aside, using it merely as part of the case for the truth, or the relative truth, of the story of Helen. The writer believes that Helen did exist. Whether she was abducted, whether she went willingly, whether the gathering of the Greek chiefs took place immediately after her abduction, or whether these are entirely separate stories, it is impossible to say. It is conceivable that Helen was abducted and was later recovered by her husband, while a hundred years before or later the Trojan war took place. It may be that there was no connection between the two stories, but it is likely that part of the story is true, because it is not likely that Homer (or the school of Homer) could compose anything so complex, using one or two persons whose historical existence is comparatively established, without using a certain amount of fact. Much in the legend of Helen may be untrue, but much must be historical. Since the story is immortal, there is no great objection to treating it as true throughout in basing an account of it on the *Iliad* of Homer and upon Virgil's *Æneid*.

The birth of Helen is conveyed to us as are so many genealogies in Greek literature. Being beautiful, she was inevitably the daughter of one of the gods. According to the legend we find in Greece a king of Sparta called Tyndareus, who had for wife the beautiful Leda. Jupiter, that most uxorious Olympian divinity, saw Leda, and, smitten with love of her, sought to obtain possession of her. Here we encounter the Greek point of view as to the gods: the conception is not one of an omnipotent god, but of a human, a thoroughly anthropomorphic god. The Greeks imagined Jupiter as capable of falling in love like an ordinary human being, of encountering difficulties, and of triumphing over these difficulties by ingenuity.

The gods in the end always prevailed over men, but occasionally man acquires a protector, namely another god, and it is out of the conflict of these gods that tragedy arises. Mars may not agree with Jupiter; Juno may be jealous of Venus. (The present writer uses indifferently the Greek and the Roman names of these gods.)

Therefore Jupiter was in his amours occasionally driven to stratagem. For instance, he triumphed over Danæ by introducing himself into her chamber as a shower of gold, a fact which reveals in the Greeks a certain acquaintance with one side of feminine nature. In the case of Leda, Jupiter used a different subterfuge; he transformed himself into a swan, and Leda, attracted by the beautiful bird, found that its wings were the arms of a lover. Of this passion was born Helen, who passed as the daughter of Tyndareus, was brought up in the royal palace, and inherited a great destiny.

She inherited also a curse—the curse of beauty. It is unfortunate that Homer gives no exact description of Helen: the word "fair" means "beautiful" rather than golden-haired, and we know nothing of her proportions or of her colouring. But Rossetti's picture of Helen certainly approximates to reality, though it is merely the product of the painter's creative imagination. Rossetti shows us Helen with long golden hair, deeply waved, blue eyes lying far apart under a low brow; the nose is deliciously formed, and

L. David

PARIS AND HELEN

the mouth represents a perfect bow; the neck and the jaw are broad, the hands unforgettable, with their fingers that taper into points. Indeed it is likely that Helen was fair. A vast majority of the Greek women were dark; the average Greek eye was brown. Therefore Helen could not have asserted herself as the beauty of all the ages unless she differed from her contemporaries. Therefore she must have been fair.

Very early the beauty which was to be fatal to her asserted itself in her life, since at the age of fourteen she was abducted by Theseus, King of Athens. According to the legend she bore him a daughter, Iphigenia, who was later to make romantic history of her own. However, Helen did not remain the wife of Theseus. Either she escaped or was recovered in war, for a few years later we find her once more at the court of Sparta under the sway of her legal father, Tyndareus. Many suitors sought the hand of Helen, attracted by her beauty and by the power of the King of Sparta. Among them were Patroclus, the friend of Achilles, no doubt great in beauty, and Menelaos, son of Atreus, King of Mycenæ. It is conceivable that games were held, since the Greeks attached much importance to prowess in the field. Patroclus, as we shall see later, was a bold warrior, but so was Menelaos. Possibly Menelaos triumphed, for soon after we find him the husband of Helen, and the father of her child, Hermione.

Here intervenes already a fact which goes towards buttressing the theory outlined at the beginning of this chapter, and according to which it is unlikely that the Greeks would have waged war for the sake of

a woman: nothing in the records shows that the value of Helen was in the least impaired by her relations with Theseus. Though she has lived with Theseus and borne him a child, she is equally desired by Patroclus and by Menelaos. They attached no importance to chastity. Later in her history, when she has spent half her lifetime with Paris; when she has been wedded to his brother, Deiphobus, she is taken back by her husband, and lives with him, possibly for many years. All this confirms the present writer in his belief that for a matter so trifling as the loss of a woman the Trojan war would not have been engaged.

Presumably Helen lived with Menelaos for several years; so far as can be calculated she must have married him at the age of sixteen and lived with him until the age of twenty-five or twenty-six. This we know from her age at the time of the fall of Troy, and from the time which expired between her flight and her recovery by her husband. We know nothing of Helen's life with Menelaos. Presumably it was the life of a Greek woman of good position, submissive to her husband, entertained by her slaves, the years containing no event worth recording. But while Helen was living with Menelaos the fates were spinning their thread, and this thread was to produce as tangled a mesh as could be woven. That mesh took the shape of Paris.

Some years before the birth of Helen King Priam of Troy and his wife Hecuba had a child which was cursed from birth because Hecuba dreamt that she would bring forth, not a child, but a torch that should burn Troy. It was a prophetic dream, though Paris

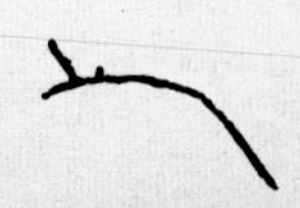

never set his hand to the walls of the city ; he was to bring disaster upon it and to cast it into ruins. Thus, when Paris was born Priam and Hecuba wept over their child, but, fearing the wrath of the gods, sought to avert it by quenching this torch that was doomed to burn their city. They exposed Paris upon a height, and he was not seen again.

But Paris did not die. The Greek myth gives him as a nurse a she-bear, just as the Roman myth gave a wolf-mother to Romulus and Remus. In fact, Paris was saved by some kindly peasants, who brought him up as their own child, and later made him into a shepherd. Here enters an element which is foreign to the story of Helen, namely the love which the nymph Œnone shed upon Paris. It is one of those delicate duels between men and immortals in which Greek literature is so fecund. We have a vision of Paris shepherding his sheep, and as he walks along a glade, playing upon a pipe a tune which he has overheard in the wind where plays Pan, drawn by the magic of his music, a nymph shows through the bushes a flash of white flank and laughing eyes, a strand of hair shining like a cobweb in the dawn. The sweet nymph has the secret of healing. She throws at the feet of Paris love, comfort, and she would cast away her immortality so that she might not survive him.

For Paris is beautiful, and the lines of Andrew Lang bring before us the proud youth that was to be a prince.

Beside King Diocles there sat a man
  Of all men mortal sure the fairest far,
For o'er his purple robe Sidonian
  His yellow hair shone brighter than the star

Of the long golden locks that bodeth war ;
His face was like the sunshine, and his blue
Glad eyes no sorrow had the spell to mar
Were clear as skies the storm hath thunder'd through.

And his beauty was to bring disaster, death, to him, for it was to mark him out from among all mortals, to call down upon him the eyes of the gods who exalt and who abase. It happened that King Peleus was betrothed to Thetis, the marine goddess who rises from the waves, fair as Aphrodite. In view of the royal state of Peleus, the wedding feast was noble, and was bruited over the whole of the known world—that is, the little world about the Ægean Sea.

To this feast were bidden the mortals and the gods. Among these immortals were Venus, Hera, and Pallas the wise. But of the gods one was forgotten—Eris. Outraged in her dignity, Eris came uninvited to the wedding feast, and to avenge herself threw among the guests an apple upon which she had inscribed : "To the fairest." We may imagine the stir that went about the assembly when this inscription was read, how mortal and immortal women looked into the mirrors of burnished silver, and into the more eloquent mirrors of their lovers' eyes. Almost immediately speculation must have turned to quarrel, and the three goddesses—Venus, Pallas, and Hera—confronted one another demanding that all should recognise their superior fairness.

The story of the apple of discord has been told not only by Homer but by Apuleius ; it appears in the Middle Ages in *The Romance of the Rose* ; filters to Congreve and to Tennyson ; humanity always being seduced by the idea that it may determine the greatest fairness.

However, the question proved impossible of solution. We may imagine confused argument, judges set up and then cast down, possibly fighting. At last the smoke clears away, and we now hear that it is decided that the proclamation of the most beautiful woman shall be made by the most beautiful man, and that man is Paris. The shepherd playing his pipes is suddenly exalted as judge among gods.

Here again we strike the simple Greek conception of the gods: like human beings, they cheat. The three goddesses offer bribes to the shepherd so that he may be moved to proclaim fair her who is most corrupt. And it is Venus who wins this ugly competition: she offers Paris the possession of the most beautiful woman in the whole world. Because Paris is young, because the romance of the unknown woman draws him, he forgets Œnone, accepts the bribe of Venus. Whereupon Venus, whom at this stage we should more properly call Aphrodite, directs his steps to Sparta and to the palace of King Menelaos.

It is conceivable that Helen and Paris fell in love at first sight, for the young shepherd had the bearing of a prince, and it is likely that Menelaos was older. Also, Paris had no difficulty in causing himself to be recognised as a prince. His beauty, his air of breeding, his prowess in sports, all this shed about him a halo, to which was added the infinitely more powerful diadem set upon his brow by grateful Aphrodite. Here it is interesting to note that to a certain extent, according to the *Iliad*, to a greater extent according to Andrew

Lang, Helen resisted this fatal passion. She wished to be a faithful wife, and indeed the nineteen years which she spent with Paris appear to have been wholly faithful. Not a word is said to suggest that Helen ever turned towards another lover. But she could not resist the thrall which Aphrodite laid upon her. Andrew Lang expresses this well:

> But Helen leap'd from her fair carven bed
> Like some tormented thing that fear makes bold,
> And on the ground she beats her golden head
> And pray'd with bitter moanings manifold.
> Yet knew that she could never move the cold
> Heart of the lovely Goddess, standing there,
> Her feet upon a little cloud, a fold
> Of silver cloud about her bosom bare.

But Aphrodite was merciless, even though Helen pleaded pitifully:

> "Behold my heart is purer than the plume
> Upon the stainless pinions of the swan,
> And thou wilt smirch and stain it with the fume
> Of all thy hateful lusts Idalian.
> My name shall be a hissing that a man
> Shall smile to speak, and women curse and hate,
> And on my little child shall come a ban,
> And all my lofty home be desolate."

The merciless Aphrodite answered that she loved Helen well, that her fate was written, that she must abandon Menelaos, abandon her child Hermione. She must go to Paris. Then the vision faded away, and Helen, laden with guilt, sick with love, poisoned as truly as was Titania with the love-drops that were poured into her eyes, took ship and with Paris fled to Troy.

It is interesting to note that the Greeks hesitated, that they did not forthwith arm and recapture their most precious possession. They first sent an embassy to Troy, demanding the restoration of Helen and of her property. But King Priam and his son Paris found themselves bound in honour as well as in desire. Priam could not surrender the fugitives, could not deliver into the hands of the revengeful Greeks the son who had come back to him, snatched by fate from death, come back with a woman whose beauty was so blinding that Priam's knees were as water. He could not resist her charm any more than she herself could resist the enthralment of Aphrodite.

The expedition was preparing for nine years. One may imagine that the siege of Troy was a considerable matter. Here was an old city, no doubt well fortified, containing a large and industrious population, granaries, wells; a city garrisoned by numerous and barbarous troops, led, not by Paris the shepherd, but by well-known warriors, such as Hector and Æneas. However, the doom of Troy had been sealed by its treacheries, and by the rivalry of the Greeks. Tribal hostility was set aside, and in these nine years an army was drilled and equipped.

At last there landed upon the Trojan shore the Greek horde. We know nothing of its armament, or of its valour, but we do know that it was more powerfully led than the Trojan army. Among the chiefs were Agamemnon, the king of kings, brave Idomeneus, Achilles, the bravest of all (made, no doubt, all the braver by the fact that his mother had dipped him into the Styx, thus making him invulnerable except in the heel), the equally brave Ajax, and Patroclus, friend of Achilles. With the Greeks went intellect as well as valour, namely the counsel of old Nestor, who had seen much war—above all, the brains of Ulysses, subtlest of all, confirmed liar, play-actor, most Machiavellian of all the Greeks.

It would be wearisome to detail at length the course of this long war. Homer affords us mainly an account of single combats, which accords with his aristocratic point of view. For instance, soon after the arrival of the Greeks, Menelaos challenged Paris to single combat. This offer Paris rejected, much to the wrath of gallant Hector, who charged him with being more beautiful than valiant. Paris appears to have tried to shelter himself by diplomatically remarking that love and beauty are gifts of the gods equally with bravery. He undertook to fight for the possession of Helen, but the latter appears to have been incensed by her lover's apparent cowardice. She curses him. And it is presumed that Hector, who was always a friend of Helen, though no lover, was amused by this, and that he undertook to protect her against any evil that might impend.

Already, therefore, there is disunion at Troy, disunion between the lovers themselves. Cassandra fills the palace with the forebodings that haunt her; the people are restless, realising that the gods have, by bringing Helen into their walls, laid upon their shoulders a wrath which they fear. And they fear still more the arms of the Greeks. The story develops, a constant tale of battle. The gallant Hector is slain by Achilles, who drags his body round the walls of

Troy, while the tears of old King Priam flow and mingle with those of Andromache, Hector's widow. The war continues, and no doubt many assaults are delivered in vain upon the walls of Troy. Still the siege is not relaxed, though nothing is said of provisions, from which one may conclude that Troy was so placed as to be isolated with difficulty. Doubtless, food and reinforcements easily reached Troy from the interior.

Achilles, invulnerable save in the heel, was slain by an arrow which pierced him just where fate had not armoured him. Disaster struck both camps, and yet there was chaos in Troy, not only because the Trojans feared the Greeks as because they feared the gods. They were fated, and the old prophecy held good—the son of King Priam had come back to light a torch and burn down the walls of Troy. Thus one can understand the revolt of the Trojans, who realised that Helen was accursed, and sought to expel with her the evil that stood within their walls. Thus the people proposed to Paris that he should surrender Helen to the Greeks. Perhaps Paris, after so many years, no longer loved Helen with his heart, but the enthralment of Aphrodite was too strong. He could not surrender her if he would. Rather would he risk the destruction of Troy. And still the war continues.

The Greek camp lies before the city, another city of its own where women live as well as soldiers, where children are born, where social life springs up—a counter-Troy. And it seems clear that never will they resign the grip they have set upon the city. But with time terminations hurry, and the disaster which was promised comes to pass.

Philoctetes was an archer, armed with the poisoned arrows of Hercules. One of these arrows found its mark in the body of Paris, and while Helen, her beautiful eyes raining tears, her golden hair disordered, flung herself raving by his couch, he sickened. He was doomed to die, though the kindly nymph Œnone might have healed him. But Œnone could not forgive his desertion of her for Helen ; though a nymph, she was human enough to believe that her lover could have resisted the call of Aphrodite if only he had loved her enough. So she would not heal him, and only when Paris was dead did a mist of remorse rise in Œnone, hiding the treachery of Paris. She would have cured him then, when he lay dead, but it was too late. In her repentance she flung herself upon his funeral-pyre and mingled her ashes with his.

And now indeed the situation of Helen was terrible. Much blood had been shed, much pain endured by a population weary of war, which did not desire war, which would gladly have been rid of the Greeks, and which naturally blamed Helen for all these disasters. Paris, who loved her, was dead ; Hector, who had protected her, was dead. King Priam was old, and Cassandra walked the palace, a figure of woe and of revenge, tearing her hair, wringing her hands, mingling her lamentations with those of old Queen Hecuba. In those days the palace must have been a place of terror, animated by the tears of the Trojan women who could look forward only to death or to captivity.

But even so the thrall of Helen was strong, though she was over forty. The two sons of King Priam, Helenus and Deiphobus, claimed her hand, and no doubt according to the Greek primitive custom, which corresponds to that of many other tribes, Helen could not stay unwed, but must marry a brother-in-law. She chose Deiphobus.

At last Troy fell. It did not fall by assault, but by the subtle shaft of Ulysses. It is said that Ulysses in the guise of a beggar had some years before penetrated Troy, confronted Helen, and sought to gain her complicity to the surrender of the city. In those days she was bemused, and she refused, but it was Ulysses who finally compassed the fall of Troy. To him we owe the stratagem of the wooden horse, which the Greeks erected upon the shore; then they withdrew with their fleet, so that the Trojans might believe that the siege was raised and the victory theirs. At this point one may question whether the loyalty of Helen was with the Trojans or with the Greeks, for it is said that with Deiphobus she walked round the wooden horse and that she suspected a stratagem. According to this account, believing that Greeks had concealed themselves within the horse, she called to them, imitating the voices of their wives, so that they might betray themselves. But Ulysses the wise stopped their mouths.

However, whether Helen sought to expose the Greeks or not, the warriors appeared from the flanks of the wooden horse, and flung the gates of Troy open, poured into the city, sword in one hand, torch in the other, followed soon after by the horde of the returning Greeks. Then comes the familiar picture of a sacked city, men-at-arms rushing through palace and hovel, putting to the sword men, women, children. We have a vision of the broad marble corridors of the palace, lit up as in daylight with the flames of the burning city. Trojan girls are captured and dragged out by the hair, Greek soldiers loot the treasure-chests, Priam is killed by Pyrrhus, son of Achilles—and all this is but a detail when we conceived the rush of Menelaos, followed by his soldiers, seeking in the burning palace the woman who was stolen from him, the woman for whom so much blood has been poured out. Doubtless he intends to slay her, and perhaps she is driven out. According to Andrew Lang:

> Then Helen through the camp was driven and thrust,
> Till even the Trojan women cried in glee,
> "Ah, where is she in whom was set thy trust,
> The Queen of love and laughter, where is she?
> Behold the last gift that she giveth thee,
> Thou of the many loves! to die alone,
> And round thy flesh for robes of price to be
> The cold close-clinging raiment of sharp stone."

But, in fact, the most likely account is that Helen, released from the thrall of Aphrodite by the death of Paris, sought only to save herself. Though he was in a sacked city, the gutters of which were running with blood and the walls striped with flame, Deiphobus had been fighting many a long day, and now, exhausted, he lay in his chamber. Thus we may imagine Menelaos rushing towards Helen, sword in hand, determined to end with her life an epic of blood and shame. But Helen holds him back, and says to him: "Would you not protect your own honour first? I will lead you." The Greek chief is simple and rough; his wrath is easily turned by perplexity. He allows Helen to lead him to the chamber where her husband lies, and slays him.

And Helen is spared. She is spared perhaps because she is still so beautiful that a man's hand must turn against himself if he raise it against her. She is spared because equally with Menelaos and Paris she has been the victim of the gods. Though Menelaos is minded to shed her blood for all that she has shed, he cannot bring himself to this. She is too beautiful. So he forgives her. Or rather he overlooks her. He does not essentially care whether she gave herself to Paris and to Deiphobus. He has recovered her—not only the pleasure of her, but the sense of mastery which she affords him. Helen takes ship with him, and sails back to Greece, leaving behind her the memory of the smoking ashes where lies Paris.

The tragic story unfolds. Ajax slays himself, humiliated by his defeat at the hands of Achilles. Agamemnon, on his return to Greece, is murdered by Ægisthus with the connivance of his own wife, Clytemnestra. Nestor ends his days in peace, while Ulysses wanders many years upon the sea, striving to regain Ithaca and his wife Penelope. "The captives and the kings depart," and the story ends upon Helen once again a queen, still loved, still dominating by eternal beauty. Of her Andrew Lang says:

> But Helen was a Saint in Heathendom,
> A kinder Aphrodite; without fear
> Maidens and lovers to her shrine would come
> In fair Therapnæ, by the waters clear
> Of swift Eurotas.

According to one account she killed herself, finding that her beauty was passing. Others say that she was dethroned by her stepsons after the death of Menelaos, and that she was killed by Polyxo and her maids, disguised as furies, to whom she had fled for protection, who hunted and drove her about, recalling to her all the agony she had brought upon the world by the fatal gift of beauty.

Indeed Helen represents to us one of the most definite Greek convictions—that fate is jealous and makes men pay for anything it gives. It was this feeling made Polycrates, the tyrant of Samos, cast a ring into the waters, so that he might suffer and thus propitiate fate which had made him too powerful and too happy. But Helen could not make such a treaty with the jealous gods. They had given her a beauty which still glows immortal, though the dust of thousands of years lies upon the dust of Helen. "Dust hath closed Helen's eyes," as Thomas Nashe puts it. All those upon whom she looked perished as surely as were turned to stone those who gazed upon the face of Medusa. Yet she lives in our imagination, a memory so gracious that few men would to-day refuse the risk and the delight of a dream which for one short hour could make them by the sight of Helen as exalted and as happy as was once the faithless lover of Œnone.

BIBLIOGRAPHY

Press translation of *The Iliad*, by Lang, Leaf & Myers.

Pope's translation of *The Iliad*.

Helen of Troy, by Andrew Lang.

J. A. Simonds's *Greek Studies*.

Classical Greek Literature, by Mahaffy.

Virgil's *Æneid*.

THE CARLYLES

IV. THE CARLYLES

PAIN WITHOUT PASSION

CHARLES KINGSLEY, in an æsthetic mood, remarked that not the house you live in matters, but the house opposite; the present writer, in investigating the married life of Thomas and Jane Carlyle, would perhaps have done well to visit the house opposite, but, so far as recollection goes, opposite stands a blank wall, and this may have governed the matrimonial miseries of two people of great distinction. Nevertheless, one cannot help thinking that 24 Cheyne Row, in Chelsea, where the Carlyles spent most of their joint lives, is full of suggestions. People do not live many years in a house unless it corresponds with the temperament of one of them. And sometimes they make it into a symbol of their unity. If that is so, then one understands much of the misery of the Carlyles.

The house in Chelsea is a Georgian building, erected at the end of the eighteenth century. It is of red brick and has small windows. Upon the ground floor we find a dining-room and another small room, which gives upon a garden. It is a tiny garden, with a lawn as large as a couple of big carpets; two trees live along the grass. Walls everywhere. It is a prison-yard, where one can imagine the tumultuous spirit of Carlyle beating itself against the confining space, Mrs. Carlyle weeping alone.

We go up the staircase to a half-landing, where Carlyle often sat, looking out into the prison-yard, and reach on the first floor a drawing-room, giving into a very small room which was Mrs. Carlyle's. It is a tragic little room, with a window facing east. It is half-filled by a large bed under a canopy, a bed so large that it touches the mantelpiece and leaves hardly any room to move in; how eloquent! Behind is a small room that was once a powder-closet for garnishing with white dust the hair of fine ladies in the days of George III.

Above, the front is occupied by a spare-room of extreme Victorian hideousness, where once slept Emerson. Behind is Carlyle's room, larger than his wife's, and, again, thus eloquent. Here too a canopied bed and a powder-closet.

But where we understand at once the life of the Carlyles is when we reach the extremities of the house, the kitchen and the attic. The kitchen, as was universal in those days, occupies the lower ground floor, and is badly lit through a narrow area. In the days of the Carlyles no artificial light was available, and no water flowed through a pipe; all water came from a well. What is still more surprising is that there is no oven, except a small iron chest two feet square. The jack can still be seen, and an iron hook from which, by means of a chain, was hung meat to roast. That was the domestic equipment with which Mrs. Carlyle, a fine lady by temperament, had to give parties.

The other extreme of the house, the attic, is still more eloquent. That was Carlyle's work-room, a large space with a sloping roof, and here we discover Carlyle. Noise had always been intolerable to him; his nerves were always fretted. So he devised the extraordinary expedient of a sound-proof room. Within the sloping roof he erected a set of vertical walls, blocked the window by a door, and against the skylight built heavy wooden shutters. He was always in difficulties, because he liked ventilation and could exclude sound only by excluding light and air. But still, often in his furies he closed the aperture, and we can imagine him "cribbed, cabined, and confined," shut away from the world of sound, the world of air, the world of sight—shut away from Mrs. Carlyle, who sits alone in her drawing-room, or struggles in her kitchen.

Can anything be more graphic than this contrast? The writer felt it intensely, because he last visited Cheyne Row on a Carlylean day. Upon a yellow sky dun-coloured clouds hung menacingly, a storm brooded, while in the west a touch of flame rose from the sunset. The house was filled with splendid gloom under which ran secret warmth. Oh, sea-green incorruptible! thy bloody ghost, bearing a severed head, walked well in such an atmosphere, in such a dark and stifling air that promised the storm, promised the rain, rain, rain from a weeping heaven as tears from a woman's eyes, while the man, desolate and inflamed, sits behind one wall and yet another wall—wall upon wall—walled up against emotion, with shutters drawn above his head, shuttered against emotion, and silence about him as he writes in a spume of passion, while with hands that tremble he clutches thoughts "fingent and fictile," in an hour close and fuliginous which shrouds him, mantles him against emotion.

Yes, the home of the last of the rhetoricians leads to rhetoric, and if only it had been inhabited by the great man and by a large, plump, good-tempered cook, we should have of Carlyle all the greatness and no domestic tragedy. Carlyle was rather akin to Strindberg, who insisted upon marrying distinguished and intellectual women, and then expected them to mend his socks. Strindberg told the truth in his *Confession of a Fool*, but Carlyle could never have applied to himself such a word: he was Scotch. Just as he should have married a good cook, Jane Welsh Carlyle should have married an actor, a financier, an Italian brigand—something coloured and variable. But the little god of love is a practical joker, and it was a sinister jest he achieved when in 1821 he brought the son of a workman, the dour, Calvinistic Carlyle, face to face with that gay, sceptical, eighteenth-century sprite, Jane Welsh.

Jane Welsh was ill-prepared by heredity for a dull life. On one side she descended from John Knox, the fierce Protestant who had pursued Mary Stuart with the epithets of "Jezebel," and "adultress"; on the other, through a grandmother, she was a gipsy. An explosive compound, passion on both sides, and on one side a tortured passion. As a child she showed her spirit by fighting a boy with her fists; she crawled across the ledge of Nungate ridge, quite willing to break her neck. Though her mother would have preferred her to be a young lady, achieving samplers and saying to men, "Oh, you naughty creature!"

J. M. Whistler

THOMAS CARLYLE

her father encouraged Jane's mind, which was a good one. She begged to learn Latin, and at the age of nine could translate Virgil. (She is much akin to George Sand, but she did not have George Sand's opportunities.) She learnt mathematics for pleasure. She spoke French and Italian. When Carlyle met her she was a bright, attractive girl, infinitely superior to the average of her period.

According to Mr. T. P. O'Connor, in his admirable sketch of the Carlyles in *Some Old Love Stories*, she was of ardent imagination and of ardent senses rather than of tender heart. Mr. O'Connor considers that she was a *femme passionée* rather than a *femme sentimentale*. It should also be noted that, according to Mrs. Ireland, "she was not apt to attribute lofty and beautiful motives to anyone." Mr. O'Connor records that she had a tongue, and a pen, biting, witty, and harsh, that she was a spoilt beauty. All this was mediocre preparation for a marriage with Carlyle, a man who saw a joke at leisure, and when he saw it doubted its propriety.

Jane Welsh also differed from her future husband in so far as she was vigorously attracted to men, while we know of only two cases where Carlyle looked upon a woman and found her fair. She was attracted to Benjamin B., as she calls him, and says delightfully when she met him with a river between them: "I durst not make any effort to attract his attention, though, had my will been consulted in the matter, to have met him *eye to eye* and *soul to soul* I would have swum, ay, swum across at the risk of being dosed in water-gruel for a month to come."

Then there is George Rennie, of whom she says: "Oh, wretch, I wish I could hate him, but I can't." Also Jane expects too much. She has read *La Nouvelle Héloïse*, delights in the heroes of Rousseau, so romantically vicious, so viciously romantic, so low in their elevation. She wants a husband like Wolmar, and prettily gives herself away in a letter where she names George Rennie, James Aitken, Robert Macturk, James Baird, Robby Angus—and maybe others, her memory fails her. The diary of Carlyle holds no such revelations.

On the other hand, there was one similarity between Carlyle and Jane Welsh: both were crossed in love. In her case the man was Edward Irving, whom doubtless she loved as she never learnt to love Carlyle.

Irving was tall and handsome, a master at the school of Haddington where Jane Welsh was educated. He also gave her private lessons, and it is certain that he loved her as entirely as she loved him. He was a curiously attractive, rapturous person, and something of his temperament may be gauged from the fact that ultimately he became a minister, and declared himself assured of the second advent of Christ. Expelled from the Presbyterian Church, he formed the Holy Catholic Apostolic Church, founded mainly on the Apocalypse, holding that angels walk the earth in human form, that saints are snatched up to Heaven, and that upon the faithful descends the gift of tongues as did flames upon the heads of the apostles. It is worth noting that though she loved him Jane Welsh mocked. Many years later she remarked tersely that if she had married Irving there would have been no gifts of tongues.

But all was against their union: not only was he in the awkward position of master and pupil, but he was engaged to a Miss Martin. Finding himself in love with Jane Welsh, he begged Miss Martin to give him his release. This was refused; Irving and Jane Welsh parted, and Irving's marriage with Miss Martin made misery for both. We know from Jane Welsh's letters how much she suffered from this early loss, to which was added the loss of her father, the man who had procured her education, who had encouraged her ambitions. She was together bereft of protector and of lover, and then she met Carlyle. The irony of their matrimonial history lies in this fact: Carlyle was brought to Haddington by Edward Irving.

Who was this Carlyle, who was at once to fall in love with Jane Welsh, and to bring her so much misery? An early portrait of Carlyle shows us a curious, wistful face, rather lean, with a long nose, a slightly drooping underlip, and the saddest eyes—eyes that dream, the eyes of something that has been hurt. And one wonders whether the aggressiveness of Carlyle is not actually a spirit of revenge, a resentment of early poverty, early ill-treatment. He was an idealist, therefore he suffered from the world, therefore he fled the world; he had imagined it as better than it is, and hated it because it was not good enough. He was born at Ecclefechan, a Scottish village, in 1795, and was therefore five years older than Jane Welsh. His father was a mason, and, as often happens among Scottish artisans, a man of a certain education who felt respect for learning. He was deeply Calvinistic, independent; in every way a fine type, but a harsh one. He was not unkind to Thomas, but he could not bring him up in comfort, even though he ultimately prospered as a farmer.

Young Carlyle went to school, and there we find one of the keys of his character: he was immensely self-conscious, sensitive, so much so that he was called "Tom the Tearful," and was bullied by the other boys. He was unhappy there, constantly unhappy, because he was of a stock too delicate for the contacts which were forced upon him. Later, at Edinburgh University, where his father sent him because he was ambitious, we find Carlyle suffering from another kind of pain: he is lonely. He has no money, no social connections, no social graces, and our vision of him is that of a young man shut up in his room, as he will later be in an attic, reading, reading—poetry, biography, science, philosophy—greedily, a young man without a bond with life, except through the pages of books. And he is intensely ambitious. He writes to Thomas Murray:

"Ever since I have been able to form a wish, the wish of being known has been the foremost. Oh, Fortune! bestow coronets and crowns and principalities and purses, and pudding and power, upon the great and noble and fat ones of the earth. Grant me that, with a heart unyielding to thy favours and unbending to thy frowns, I may attain to literary fame."

He wants to write, but he must teach, because that is the only way he can make a living. At once he encounters tragedy, namely love for Margaret Gordon, a girl better bred, better placed than himself. Though she admired him, she would not marry him, and her remarks exhibit a picture of Carlyle: "Cultivate the milder dispositions of the heart, subdue the mere extravagant visions of the brain. Genius will render you great. May virtue render you beloved. Remove the awful distance between you and other men by kind and gentle manners. Deal gently with their inferiority, and be convinced that they will respect you as much and like you more."

If Carlyle had taken this advice he might have been a happier man. But he was too hot, too self-satisfied. Forgoing Margaret Gordon, he retires to Kirkcaldy and begins to write. Already he suffers from dyspepsia, which is to pursue him all his life, and perhaps to explain his agonies better than his circumstances. Always he is alone, and always he suffers.

"I was entirely unknown in Edinburgh Circles; solitary, eating my own heart, misgivings as to whether there shall be presently anything else to eat, fast losing health, a prey to numerous struggles and miseries . . . three weeks without any kind of sleep, from impossibility to be free from noise . . . wanderings through mazes of doubt, perpetual questions unanswered, etc." And yet he could find no remedy. In fact, he loses faith in the God he has inherited from his father, not so much because he suffers as because he treats religion like a mathematical theorem. Yet he makes a few friends, and Irving is one of these. Finally, he meets Jane Welsh, and the current of his life is turned awry.

There is no space in this short chapter to make a complete picture of Carlyle as a literary man, but one should record first the encyclopædic knowledge of the man, his immense accumulation of historical learning. One should also note his natural affinity with Germany, the talent which enabled him to give Goethe to the English language. One should also observe a sort of covert anti-Christianity, which perhaps he obtained from Gibbon. And one should observe the corresponding tendency, namely the admiration for man, which he has denied God. He was a hero-worshipper, and the book where he embodies that point of view is more Carlylean than any other.

He would not accept that a period makes the man, that a great emergency, such as war or political unrest, drags the great man out of obscurity ; he believed that it is the man who makes history, that history is not the long struggle of mankind towards peace and happiness, but a sort of arena, where colossal figures are hurled together, Frederick the Great, Napolean—and Carlyle. His vision of the universe is rather akin to that of Homer and of Wagner, a sort of battle among the Titans to decide which one shall challenge the gods.

It was this young man who had known nothing but poverty, obscurity, hard work, and intoxicating ideas, this young man in whose veins flowed the harshest, most Calvinistic blood, who confronted Jane Welsh.

Whether Carlyle loved her we do not, shall never know, because nothing in his life shows any sacrifice for her, any thought for her. There is even little evidence that she appealed to him as a woman. No doubt he was seduced by her mind, by her brightness ;

he had met few women intimately, and most were commonplace. Here was a creature of twenty, able to contradict him, and for a moment to arrest his thought. Here was a girl interested in the things he cared for, capable of Latin, informed in Euclid. Four days after he met her he began to write to her, and it is half-pathetic to think of this meeting over exercise books.

The love-letters of Thomas Carlyle and Jane Welsh have been collected; they extend over five years, during which Carlyle had to struggle not only against the shade of Irving, but against a natural distaste on the part of Jane Welsh. One may suspect that he revolted her, that his brutality of mind, and, above all, his dramatic vision of history and of life, were foreign to her intensely critical, to her cynical attitude. She was the learned and mocking eighteenth century, while he was the bellowing and moral nineteenth. No picture of the Carlyles can be complete unless we add to it a few extracts from this correspondence. For instance, she writes to him:

> "I have read the tragedies. I thank you for them. They are Byron's: need I praise them? I have also read your eloquent history of *Faust*. For it too I thank you."

In the same letter she discourages his over-ardent expressions of friendship. It is as if she were afraid. Still the correspondence continues, because evidently there is in Carlyle's mind something that lures the girl, something which she cannot forgo, no doubt because her cultivated father is dead, because Irving has drawn away, and because her active mind demands some mental food. At the same time she warns him, as if she begged him to give her rest and not force her to consider her own feelings.

She says:

> "I am not at all the sort of person you and I took me for. I begin to think that I was actually meant by nature to be a fine-lady. My friends, that is my acquaintances, have told me this all along; but I would not believe them. For the last month, however, I have shown lamentable symptoms of a tendency that way: I have spent all my time in riding on horse-back, dressing three times a day, singing Italian airs, and playing at shuttlecock! Dear Sir, what will cure me?"

To which Carlyle apparently replies by asking whether she has entirely abandoned the idea of translating *Don Karlos*. He goes on to suggest that he and Jane Welsh should produce every fortnight, for mutual inspection, a given number of verses upon subjects chosen by themselves alternately. What a pin for the butterfly! But we should not laugh at this literary courtship. It may seem absurd that two young people should write to each other at length about tragedies and German histories, but we should remember that to-day many an alliance between young people of education is preluded by correspondence where they exchange views on, let us say, Marcel Proust, on Vorticist painting, and on Socialism. Just as it seems absurd

Kenneth Macleay

JANE WELSH CARLYLE

to us to-day that the Prince Consort should have read Hallam's *Constitutional History* to Queen Victoria, it seems absurd that Carlyle and Jane Welsh should communicate on Goethe. But we do these things too, and we love each other all the same. Though the correspondence is cold, it must be recorded that there is no intrinsic objection to literary correspondence between people who are attracted to each other.

But already they irritated each other. Jane Welsh wrote sharply criticising the "mystery" of the ambiguous and too-ardent expressions which he used, and warned him that she disliked these protestations as much as her mother disapproved of them. Yet there is nothing very ardent in Carlyle's letters, but the eighteen-twenties were still influenced by an earlier style, where love was declared in letters beginning: "Madam, you have doubtless long been aware of the esteem with which I venture to regard you." What was really the matter was that she was attracted by his mind and not by his person; she wanted him as a friend, but not as a lover; and she found herself in the position which so many women encounter, the problem being to retain the man's interest without giving him too much. She expresses this in several letters, and, in fact, takes up the attitude that she never will marry.

She says: "Falling in love and marrying like other Misses is quite out of the question." Whether this is dictated by the memory of Irving or aversion for Carlyle is impossible to say. She reiterates it, and Carlyle replies that he understands "her rank and prospects," being, like many a man of genius, easily impressed by superior social status and by the money which he does not possess. However, Carlyle was honest to Jane Welsh, and never approached her as so many men approach women of brains, affecting an innocent feeling and hoping that by degrees the woman will be entangled. He told her bluntly that he had "too much experience of the emptiness of sublunary things to find much enjoyment in the languishings . . . and weak delusions of boys and girls," and that he could not "degenerate into what they call a friend."

So the weary courtship continues, with Carlyle as the educator of a brilliant pupil, a natural rôle in those days, when woman was first educated into Shakespeare and the musical glasses, later into love. He writes about poetry, he enquires whether she has finished *Tasso*, Schiller's *Maria Stuart*, and *Wallenstein*. She writes back in similar style, and the correspondence would be dull if both did not write so well. On the whole, the letters are not intimate, though in 1823 they have a lovers' quarrel, and Carlyle protests that he is not angry. It is pathetic to note that Carlyle warns Jane Welsh against the approach of the black demon of melancholy.

This physician could not cure himself, and in after-life certainly provided neither "poppy nor mandragora" to soothe the unrest of his wife. But, though he does not seem to love her as an ordinary man loves an ordinary woman, he fascinates her, and he flatters her. He flatters her by constantly repeating that he has faith in her talent, that she must fulfil her ambition, that she must write, he assures her that he will yet see her "by far the most distinguished female of all I ever knew." How we understand this word "female"! Carlyle can imagine Jane Welsh more distinguished than Polly Jones, but more than Carlyle forsooth! By all the thunders that crash to a leaden doom about the eternal . . . etc.

And Jane Welsh is modest. She doubts whether she will excel "the hundreds of female novelists who infest the kingdom." She vows that her ambition is dead, buried in her father's grave, and—a little dishonestly—says nothing of Irving. So the years sear on; they meet in Edinburgh, and Carlyle writes that they must never part. Then, with tragic insight into his own character, he writes: "It seems very cruel to entice you from the sunny places you inhabit to take any share in a fate so dark and perilous." He realises that both are far too ambitious, and doubts whether they can be happy. Advancing little by little, he says that it is "dangerous and useless" to love him, to which Jane Welsh, affrighted, replies that she will never be his wife. But the habit of Carlyle gains upon her, as three years, four years, five years pass. He is her drug, as she lies buried in village life, and, realising it, writes that she could not "part from the only living soul that understands me. I would marry you to-morrow rather."

And so, because Carlyle did not understand her at all, Jane Welsh married him in 1826. She married him for the most imbecile reasons, such reasons generally having effect upon great minds: as Mr. Mencken says, "only the great are irritated by trifles." A certain Mrs. Montagu, to whom Irving had revealed the story of his love for Jane Welsh, handed the information to Carlyle, to whom Jane Welsh had often spoken bitterly or mockingly of Irving. Carlyle was greatly disturbed. Jane Welsh wrote to him confessing that once she had loved Irving passionately. Immense confusion invaded them. She had deceived Carlyle. She had not been a true friend. He, on the other hand, felt jealous of Irving, though he had gone. Perhaps it was merely that in five years he had broken down the resistance of Jane Welsh, perhaps the emotional stress brought about by this revelation made them realise that only marriage could save their friendship.

Whatever the reason, they married, terrified of marriage, each one fearing that the other might not ingeminate happiness, each one doubting his power to love.

The Carlyles were never happy, and this for reasons of a nature so intimate that very little evidence exists. What is fairly clear is that Carlyle in acquiring Jane Welsh was acquiring a companion, securing to himself the interest of a quick mind. But he was not a lover. He did not see himself as a satyr bearing upon his shoulder a captured nymph. He wanted Jane Welsh because he would have been irritated if he had not secured her. He did not look upon her as a fount of sensuous delight, or as the mother of his children. All this was incidental in his attraction; he loved her mind, and for Jane Welsh that was not enough. Ardent and romantic, she wanted to be carried away, wanted the commonplace passion that a ploughman gives a dairymaid—and Carlyle gave her German quotations.

One does not want to stress this side of the relationship, but it is practically certain that Carlyle and his wife lived forty years rather as paying guests in the same house than as lovers. What is extraordinary is that almost immediately after his marriage Carlyle, who for five years had constantly inflamed himself with this woman's mind, found no further use for her. Carlyle behaves like the ordinary sensualist who after a few days tires of a new conquest, who sees brightness in other eyes, flowers only upon other lips. But there is no sensuality in Carlyle, and it seems that he marries in a sort of weariness, having so exploited the woman's mind that no lure stays there for him.

He takes her to Craigenputtock, a house sixteen miles from any evidence of civilisation. Jane Carlyle, who had lived a life of comfort and of contact with gay and intelligent people, is imprisoned for six years on a desolate Scottish moor, and alone. For she is alone. Carlyle has been snatched up upon the steed of his art, and provides no pillion for his wife to ride. He forgets that he has an ambitious wife, and that he nurtured her ambition. He thinks only of himself and of his work. He locks himself in his room to work. He takes endless solitary walks upon the moors, while Mrs. Carlyle sits at her window watching the Scottish rain. Anyone who has visited Scotland will know the desolation of the lonely country when the rain falls day and night, for many nights and days. Though she was delicate and unused to hardship, because they were poor and had only one servant, she became Carlyle's drudge. She had naught to occupy her save the domestic round, and sometimes at night she rose from her bed to bake the bread while her husband slept.

Yet she was charming. Her picture by Gambardella, painted when she was over forty, shows such a charming face, a high, intelligent brow, the most mischievous Chinese eyes, a long, mocking nose, and a mouth which would easily become tender if only someone craved her tenderness.

At last, however, success begins to cast a trail of rose over the dark horizon of Carlyle. The couple come to London, establish themselves at Cheyne Row, and here Mrs. Carlyle finds a little relief. They have perhaps more money, and about this woman who is still young is the movement of London, and the society of men and women of intelligence, who slowly collect round the Carlyles, admiring the husband and loving the wife. It is a glowing catalogue of names hangs about the Carlyles: Browning, Emerson, Tennyson, Mazzini, many others; but they were not happy, because Carlyle in his forties suffered now more and more from the dyspepsia he had known as a boy, while his wife was worn out by her hardship in Scotland. London did not suit Carlyle; no more now than in his student days in Edinburgh could he bear noise; the rumble of the traffic, the call of the milkman, the chatter of the servants next door—all this bred in him a mad state of irritation when he raved at Mrs. Carlyle, blaming her because she was available, and rushing out of the room at last to lock himself in his sound-proof apartment, just to get away, to sit there perhaps six hours, leaving her to manage her own life.

Jane Carlyle's diary, her letters to her cousin,

Jeannie Welsh, all this bespeaks her agony of mind. She has no husband, or, if she has, he is a maddened invalid trying to force his body to achievement. And she too is to blame, for she is cutting and disagreeable; she does not always afford Carlyle the admiration he needs; she does not always agree with him; she does not bow her head when he accuses her. She does not understand that with such a man only the posture of prayer is suitable, that always she should cry "Hallelujah! hail, Carlyle!" Though in her letters we find an innocent gaiety which always charms, mainly she complains. She writes to Jeannie Welsh: "Carlyle has overset all our household arrangements here as he oversets all arrangements wherever he goes. Here we were eating lunch and dining at six!" Irritating indeed to have a man who put off lunch to compose an immortal work! We cannot quite blame Carlyle there, and Mrs. Carlyle sounds unreasonable.

Later she alludes to the "general chaos of this house where a book is swept away irrecoverably." Evidently there was a furious quarrel over this missing book which was found in Carlyle's own bookcase. No doubt, when that happened he grew still more infuriated because he was to blame. She tries to console herself; sitting, as she says, with Darwin and Mazzini with their feet on the fender, and what would a woman not give for such an experience? She makes friends, but, all through, the furies and sulks of Carlyle awake in her equal furies and more savage retorts. Always she runs to her diary or to her letters to expend accumulated irritation. She reaches fifty, she reaches sixty, and there is no alleviation.

In fact, as Carlyle becomes fashionable, as he is taken up by the powerful, she has new grounds for agony: Carlyle meets Lady Harriet Baring, a woman of position. There is in their relationship nothing in the least amorous, but Lady Harriet is young and gifted, so Carlyle, who for so many years has neglected his wife, gives Lady Harriet his companionship. He goes to Addiscombe where her family live, and Jane is forced to go too. But she is intellectually jealous; she makes herself disagreeable, does not enter into country life; thus she is unhappy at Addiscombe, and because she is unhappy she blames Carlyle. Whether Mrs. Carlyle was ever jealous of Lady Harriet in the accepted sense is uncertain. In view of Carlyle's lack of interest in the love emotion, she was not likely to suspect an intrigue, but she felt that Carlyle was giving his mind to this woman as once he had given it to her. This hurt her. Besides, she was at the time unfit to deliver sound judgment, because, being ill and sleepless, she had taken to morphia, which made her health worse, clouded her brain, and encouraged unhappy imaginations. In fact, the morphia so severely affected her that she imagined slights put upon her by Lady Harriet.

The younger woman had certainly treated Mrs. Carlyle with a certain disregard of the courtesies, because Mrs. Carlyle made herself disagreeable, took up in the drawing-room the offended and resentful air of a boy of fifteen who has been dragged to a lecture on archæology under threat of stoppage of his pocket-money. Mrs. Carlyle became so incensed by these almost imaginary slights that she had a violent scene with Carlyle, and left him to stay with some friends near Liverpool. Her letter to Mazzini, written at the time, shows that it was a serious rupture, and, though ultimately the Carlyles came together again, they came together only to end their days, and not to begin a new life.

There was no hope. They could not communicate. Carlyle produced great work after great work, *Sartor Resartus*, *Heroes and Hero Worship*, *The French Revolution*, *The History of Frederick the Great*; he had no time for the whim-whams of women. In fact when, at the age of sixty-two, Mrs. Carlyle suffered a severe accident which paralysed her on one side, Carlyle, who was then at work on his *Frederick the Great*, took hardly any notice. Perhaps he did not realise her serious condition since all he said was that she should be thankful that the accident was no worse. He must not be entirely blamed, for genius leaves little room for the natural affections: wife, child, health, all that must be burnt up in the furnace. But we should record that here Mrs. Carlyle showed herself heroic; though paralysed, she dragged herself from her bedroom into the drawing-room to see if she could help Carlyle, listen to his plan, sort his notes, if he would let her. Like a dumb beast, even then, she was craving for a little warmth out of his brain if she could not draw it from his heart.

And thus the end. Perhaps Carlyle realised at last that she was ill, for his wife, two years before she dies, writes to a friend saying that Carlyle is good to her, and that he studies her comfort as never before. But it is too late. Death is too near for amends to be made.

In 1865 Carlyle receives a great honour: he is made Lord Rector of Edinburgh University. A few days after he has delivered a triumphant rectorial address, while he is still in Edinburgh, his fame now made certain, his wife sets the full stop which ends her phrase. Because a little dog is run over in the park while she is driving, she falls back in her carriage and dies of heart-disease.

She was wasted because she had no creative talent, but only critical talent, and Carlyle was not wasted, for he could create. He had loved her once, and as the years went by he came to look upon her as a commonplace thing which was useful enough and friendly. She who should have sounded the beat of his life became the furniture of his emotions. He forgot to cherish her, and because he loved ideas too well perhaps he loved her only when she was dead. Indeed, it is worth while to quote for the ending of this long tragedy the description by John Swinton of Carlyle at his wife's grave. It is so moving that not a word need be added.

"'And Mr. Carlyle,' said the sexton, 'comes from London now and then to see this grave. He is a gaunt, shaggy, weird kind of old man, looking very old the last time he was here.' 'He is eighty-six now,' I said. 'Aye,' he repeated, 'eighty-six, and comes here to this grave all the way from London.' And I told him that Carlyle was a great man, the greatest man of the age in books, and that his name was known all over the world; but the sexton thought there were other great men lying

Daniel Maclise, R.A.

THOMAS CARLYLE

near at hand, though I told him their fame did not reach beyond the graveyard, and brought him back to talk of Carlyle. 'Mr. Carlyle himself,' said the grave-digger softly, 'is to be brought here to be buried with his wife. Aye, he comes here lonesome and alone,' continued the grave-digger, 'when he visits his wife's grave. His niece keeps him company to the gate, but he leaves her there, and she stays there for him. The last time he was here I got a sight of him, and he was bowed down under his white hairs, and he took his way up by that ruined wall of the old cathedral, and round there and in here by the gateway, and he tottered up here to this spot.' Softly spoke the grave-digger, and paused. Softer still, in the broad dialect of the Lothians, he proceeded—'And he stood here awhile in the grass, and then he kneeled down and stayed on his knees at the grave; then he bent over, and I saw him kiss the ground—aye, he kissed it again and again, and he kept kneeling, and it was a long time before he rose and tottered out of the cathedral and wandered through the graveyard to the gate, where his niece was waiting for him.'"

BIBLIOGRAPHY

The Love-Letters of Thomas Carlyle and Jane Welsh, edited by Alexander Carlyle (2 vols.).

Letters and Memorials of Jane Welsh Carlyle, edited by Froude.

New Letters and Memorials of Jane Welsh Carlyle, edited by Alexander Carlyle, with an introduction by Sir J. Crichton Browne.

Jane Welsh Carlyle; Letters to her family, 1839–1863, edited by Leonard Huxley.

Early Letters of Thomas Carlyle.

Some Old Love Stories, by T. P. O'Connor.

MARY STUART

V. MARY STUART

THE FATAL QUEEN

It is not unjust to call Mary Stuart a fatal queen, since every man who came within range of her beauty and of her intrigues soon became the prey of death or disaster. She was not an evil woman; many critics have loaded her with insults fit for Messalina, have represented her as a monster of lust, an amateur of murder. Mary, Queen of Scots, was not that; she was not as much as that. On the other hand, poets such as Schiller, such as, later, Mr. John Drinkwater, and many prose writers, have seen in Mary Stuart a figure of radiant grace, hunted and persecuted by men. She was not that; she was not as much as that.

Between these two extreme views lies the true Mary Stuart, a romantic, devout, somewhat callous, somewhat vain and selfish woman, but a woman capable of love. In other words, Mary Stuart was not in herself a great figure, but she was made great by history; notably, she was made great by one infinitely her superior in intellect, Queen Elizabeth, who hated and persecuted her from her birth to her death—a death which Mary deserved. Yet her good looks and tragic end have earned her sympathy.

The magic of Mary, Queen of Scots, was not entirely due to her beauty, though many called her beautiful. The portrait which now hangs at Holyrood is not that of a technically beautiful woman; the nose is rather too long, the forehead too high, according to our modern notions; the lips seem too thin; but the hazel eyes and the bright hair, especially the eyes with their heavy lids, are full of brooding melancholy. Also, it is evident that here is a tall woman, of rather massive proportions, with fine hands.

We know that she wrote verse and that she loved music; it is clear from many of the unfortunate pranks which she played in Edinburgh that she was gay and charming. Thus delineated by nature, and thus favoured in the mind, it is not wonderful that she drove to his destruction almost every one of the men with whom she came into contact.

At the outset it is well to explain the cause of the rivalry between Elizabeth and Mary—a rivalry in which Mary took her share. Each had claims to the English throne, or to its reversion, and each strove to bring under her sway the neighbouring realm. Mary, Queen of Scots, quartered the arms of England on her banner; Elizabeth, Queen of England, would, if she could have achieved it, have annexed to England the Scottish realm. And the irony of it is that two generations later the King of Scotland peacefully became King of the two realms—peacefully, after so much blood and so much intrigue had been expended upon the subject.

The situation was simple enough. Henry VII of England fathered Henry VIII of England and Margaret, who married James IV of Scotland. Margaret's grandchild was Mary, Queen of Scots, while Elizabeth was daughter of Henry VIII. Therefore

Painter Unknown

MARY QUEEN OF SCOTS

these two were cousins. The situation grew serious, for Elizabeth did not marry; therefore Mary, Queen of Scots, was a claiment to the English throne, and a very near claimant, since she stood so close in relationship to Elizabeth.

There were other complications, other claimants, such as Lady Jane Grey, whose claims Elizabeth easily disposed of by execution. There was Darnley, another grandson of Henry VII, who enters deeply into the sombre history of Mary, Queen of Scots. But since Darnley was merely heir to the Earl of Lennox, while Mary was royal, the field became practically narrowed between Mary and Elizabeth.

Other sources of dislike arose between the two Queens, causes which, perhaps, modelled the fate of Mary as truly as her claims to the throne. Elizabeth was nine years older than the lovely Queen, and that induced an irritation; Elizabeth was plain, almost ugly, while Mary enslaved all men; though Elizabeth was a woman of brains, it hurt her that Mary should dominate by charm while she could dominate only by power. Lastly, Elizabeth was a great intellectual figure, an acute diplomat, one of the builders of the British Empire, while Mary was vain, impetuous, and often foolish in her manœuvres, so that Elizabeth despised her. Because she despised her, looking upon her as unworthy of the position which she occupied, she came to hate her. Here, indeed, were sufficient foundations for a tragedy that lives still in the minds of men, nearly four centuries after its termination.

Mary was born in 1542, daughter of James V, King of Scotland, and of Mary of Guise, the Frenchwoman.

She appeared in a Scotland racked by wars with England, in a time of unrest, distracted by worse than wars, by the schism between the Catholics and the Protestants, ravaged also by the quarrels between the feudal chiefs, leaders of the clans, several of whom were so strong that they could aspire to the regency of Scotland, to its practical royalty. Scotland had produced no strong men as had England in Henry VIII. No king was fit to assert himself over the nobles or to establish by force a national religion. Scotland was in chaos, and it lay in the hands of a child. Here was a terrible situation, which would have needed a strong woman indeed to control it.

In such circumstances it is not wonderful that Mary of Guise should seek safety for her child. She sent Mary to the French court, where she was brought up and betrothed to the heir presumptive of the French throne. Thus, at once, Mary was thrust into diplomacy. The object of the betrothal was to unite the interests of Scotland and of France against England. England was Protestant, France was Catholic, and Scotland mainly Catholic. Obviously historic advantage lay in making common cause against the common enemy.

But Mary's upbringing at the French court was such as to create the worst possible basis for the mind of a Queen of Scotland. The Scotch were primitive—in many parts of the Highlands wild ; they were under the sway of John Knox and Presbyterianism in its puritanic form. The Scots—hating luxury, music, the graces, passionately aspiring to the clean moral life—were to be confronted with a charming young

Queen who had lived in a court where day and night was heard the sound of music, where the conversation was of gallantry and poetry, where improper stories were told in the presence of young women, where morality existed only to provide object for merriment. John Knox thundered and bade the Scotch choose between heaven and hell, while Mary wrote poetry. The concussion must be fatal. If Mary had been brought up in Scotland, especially if she had been a Presbyterian, the Scots might have rallied about her, defended her against Elizabeth, instead of dividing into factions.

Still, the first act of the drama must be played. At the age of sixteen she married the heir to the French throne, and at seventeen was Queen of France. It is only fair to say here that not only her own ambition, but that of the French, led her to folly; with her own hands she embroidered a banner bearing two crowns and the motto "A third awaits me." The two crowns were those of Scotland and France; the motto alluded to the crown of England. It was a fatal motto. Still, she was happy, she was ambitious, and she was mistress of France, since her husband, Francis II, was feeble. But his fragility ruined his wife, for he died when Mary was eighteen. She was no longer Queen of France, but merely Queen of a remote kingdom to which now she must return.

Here develops the first romantic episode, the journey to Scotland, to her own country, the government of which was in the hands of a regent. To reach Scotland the natural route lay across England, where reigned Elizabeth. Since the quarrel had not yet reached its high point, Mary asked of Elizabeth a free passage. Doubtless she expected to attach to her English Catholic nobles, and thus she already plotted against Elizabeth. But the English Queen was well informed and, a better judge of character than Mary, she refused passage unless Mary satisfied the Treaty of Leith, under which she surrendered her claims to the English crown.

Being high-spirited, Mary refused, and on a small ship found her way to Scotland, haunted by the fear that an English ship would capture her, or that she would be boarded by Protestants. It was a long and painful journey, and yet she miraculously escaped perils and landed at Leith. She was not expected, she was only half-welcomed in Edinburgh, and John Knox, the furious leader of the Presbyterians, begged the Almighty to purge the land from idolatry, never again to allow it to be polluted by one such as this Catholic Queen. There were divisions among the nobles, according to their religion; the Protestants imagined, and quite rightly, that Mary would strive to force Catholicism upon Scotland; the Catholics feared assassination. The Scottish Parliament had already established the Protestant faith, and the Queen did not belong to it.

Mary strove to be fair, appointing to her Privy Council Protestants as well as Catholics, but she would not forgo her religion; she heard mass at Holyrood, and the Presbyterian agitation ceased to be one of defence, became an attempt to force the Queen to abandon the Catholic faith.

Mary was happy enough, and foolish enough, in a

Protestant land. With her courtiers she disguised herself, wandered about Edinburgh, demanding pledges of men and eating in taverns. This was bruited about, and behaviour which might have been suitable for Bagdad, in Edinburgh proved fatal to the credit of the Queen. There was no overt revolt, but the Protestants stalked the land, attacking the church of Rome, "sullied with a thousand abominations," thus suggesting that any Catholic must be equally sullied. Thus it became essential that Mary should marry again, find a man to be her champion. Otherwise she could hardly hope to survive another revolution. Her mother had made a revolution, and the next might be bloody.

A marriage with Mary, Queen of Scots, was a complicated matter, because it involved the almost automatic enmity of England. Still, there were suitors: the King of Denmark, the King of Sweden, the Archduke Charles, and Carlos, son of Philip of Spain. Here at once diplomacy appeared, since in the sixteenth century royal marriage was a great matter deciding peace and war. Elizabeth might have tolerated an alliance with a Scandinavian king, but union between Scotland and Spain, England's hereditary enemy, was more than she could venture. She allowed it to be understood that she was opposed to such a marriage, since hostility to England was at the time not desired in Spain; since, also, Catherine de Medici, the French Queen Mother, saw in any alliance between Scotland and Spain perils that might develop, Philip did not encourage the marriage with his son, and much time passed.

Meanwhile, Elizabeth, anxious that Mary should not marry, and so produce yet another claimant to the English throne, realised that she could not prevent it. Thus, with a certain meanness of spirit, she offered her friendship to Mary, sought husbands for her. But they were not to be royal husbands. She suggested Lord Robert Dudley, her own lover, who was believed to have murdered his wife. She proposed Leicester, another of her lovers, a man of no importance. She would stifle the Scottish Queen by a low alliance. Only later did she become afraid of Darnley, future Earl of Lennox—he, too, of royal blood. In so far as concerns Mary's second marriage, Elizabeth was outwitted and foiled by the desire of the Lennox family to obtain a throne.

Mary's matrimonial chances were also complicated by her conduct. She was unfortunately too free in her regard, and men did not respect her. For instance, when she was walking in a garden a certain Captain Hepburn handed her a letter and a drawing such as he would have laid before no woman whom he respected.

Again, Chastelard, a French poet, attached himself to Mary, whom he entertained as she would be with poem and song, but whose reputation he damaged. The rumour of her relations with Chastelard had much to do with the hesitations of Spain to agree to her marriage with the heir. Chastelard was very young, he became intoxicated by Mary's beauty, and twice tried at night to penetrate into her chamber. There he was arrested, his execution inevitably following. A confession of Chastelard exists, but it holds no proof of a relationship between the Queen and the man other than that of friendship.

Elizabeth still pursued a satisfactory marriage with Mary, championing the Earl of Arran, who was a Protestant. The latter, foolishly supported by Bothwell—of whom more will be said—plotted to assassinate the Catholic Earl of Mar and Maitland of Lethington. That absurd plot led to the exile of Arran, though Bothwell was forgiven. No doubt this conspiracy, adding itself to internal unrest, produced in Mary a state of mind dictating to her that she must marry at once and obtain some support in her own country. If she could not marry a King of Spain she must marry whom she could. It was then, when she was twenty-three, that she met Darnley. Mary needed a strong man, a champion, and she met Darnley; history has its irony.

Darnley was three years younger than Mary, and was certainly endowed with attraction. He was very tall, rather thin; the picture which lies before the writer shows a rounded, plumply boyish face, with long, raised eyebrows, a mass of yellow hair under a cap. He looks stupid, conceited. History records many cases where a woman of greater parts than Mary had been attracted by a fool such as Darnley soon showed himself to be.

Whether Mary fell in love with Darnley, or whether the need for a satisfactory marriage operated in her mind, will never be clear. In view of her subsequent conduct, it is likely that she married Darnley for good political reasons, and that only one man in her life did she actually love—Bothwell. Certainly much spoke for Darnley. He was Catholic enough to be supported by the Catholic opponents of Elizabeth in England. On the other hand, he was not disagreeable to the Scottish Protestants. The Catholics were with him, and if Elizabeth opposed him he might gain the support of the Scottish Protestants. For the men of the sixteenth century were much akin to those of the twentieth : man might hold his faith strongly, but a Scot naturally elected to be against the English.

It is certain that Mary hesitated before marrying Darnley, for she had not yet given up hope of becoming Queen of Spain, but the Chastelard scandal and the weakness of the Scottish kingdom made this alliance impossible. Besides, Mary was arrayed against a woman as subtle and as unscrupulous as Elizabeth, Catherine de Medici, the dowager Queen of France, who desired for her son, Charles IX, a marriage with Elizabeth ; she naturally wished to impede the marriage of Mary, the historic enemy of Elizabeth, to the heir of the powerful crown of Spain. Catherine spread a rumour that her son was seeking the hand of Mary ; she thus intended to force Elizabeth to marry her son, and in so doing she made Mary still more distasteful to the Spanish King.

So Mary married Darnley. She married him at the last so hurriedly that she did not even wait for the Papal dispensation that could authorise her to marry her cousin. And with Darnley she was unhappy. Almost at once she discovered that the man was foolish, that he cared only for sports, dancing, merry-making with courtiers, and, above all, that his vanity was enormous. Indeed, within four months of their marriage he demanded that Mary should give him the crown matrimonial; that is to say, elevate him from the rank of consort to that of King of Scotland. It is clear that Mary could not have loved him, for she refused, and probably her own vanity was touched; she wished to be Queen alone, and not to share the rank with a man whom she elevated.

Thus she was forced to seek support in men other than her husband. One was Rizzio, the other Bothwell, and she needed them, for immediately after her marriage a Protestant rebellion arose under Moray, and was suppressed with difficulty. She needed Bothwell, for first Darnley quarrelled with her in public, demanding the crown, then shut himself up in his apartments, refusing to speak to her. Finally, he showed himself coward enough to write to the Pope, denouncing his wife for not enforcing Catholicism in Scotland. He fell into contempt: the English ambassador refused to discuss matters of state with him, and thus the foolish, vain man was exasperated into an action which was to bring into Mary's life yet another tragedy—namely, the murder of Rizzio.

Rizzio was an Italian musician who gained Mary's favour, as did all men who did not ignore the graces. He stayed at the Court, and became the Queen's secretary. He was an intelligent adviser, and supported her in her plans to restore Catholicism in her kingdom. Here was an opportunity which Darnley perceived, or, rather, he saw a chance to do an evil which would increase his self-esteem, which would make him feel himself a great man. Whether he believed that Mary was unfaithful to him with Rizzio, whether this was merely a figment of a wounded mind, one cannot tell, but Darnley did so accuse her, and went so far as to charge that the child whom Mary bore him was the child of Rizzio.

Now, by this time Darnley was ruined in public esteem, and so a small band of nobles, all rebels—Morton, Argyle, Glencairn, Boyd and others—made with his assent a covenant, intending mainly to enforce Protestantism and to recover their estates, but to murder Rizzio only as an incidental. Thus Darnley could assert himself. Leaving his minions, he forced his way into the Queen's apartments; Rizzio was seized in her presence, dragged into the next room, and stabbed in many places, while Darnley controlled Mary by force.

Mary was now practically the prisoner of the conspiracy, and she decided to escape. Here comes an irony, for Darnley, terrified by what he had done, cowed by the allies whom he had placed in power, betrayed them to her. Then, like a pullet that shelters under the hen's wing, fled with Mary to Dunbar. It is stated that even then, no doubt because he was her husband and the father of her child, she tried to invest him with her own ambitions: a Catholic revival in Scotland and defeat for Elizabeth, but Darnley, coward one day, bully the other, showed himself useless; and Mary saw that upon his arm she could not rely.

In fact, the existence of Darnley, the bar which this existence placed in the way of an alliance which would effectively defend Mary, must have become to her a haunting thought. She was tied to a worthless man, and she must have desired his death, as many wives have desired the death of their husbands. But it is not certain that she compassed it.

All that can be charged for certain against Mary is a conference with the Protestant nobles, Moray, Bothwell, Argyle, Huntly, and Maitland, where she agreed to divorce Darnley if such a divorce could be procured. The nobles offered Mary to "rid" her of Darnley, who had fled to Glasgow, fearing Morton, one of the murderers of Rizzio, the man he had betrayed, fearing those who had been his friends as much as those who had been his enemies.

In this new conspiracy Bothwell was definitely the leader, he being at last the man whom Mary needed. If she had married Bothwell instead of Darnley, her history might have been different. He was a big man, of somewhat brutal countenance; his long nose, thick mouth, large, open eyes combined in coarse effect. Mary loved him—of that we may be sure—not only because she was naturally attracted to a strong man, but because she, who had married a weakling (Francis II), and a vain fool (Darnley), ached from every atom of her nature for a man who knew what he wanted and was willing to attempt it. Also he hated England; he had never made terms with England; he had never, like the other nobles, taken with one hand from Scotland, with the other from England. He was safe, and Mary fled to safety.

So this young woman, then only twenty-four, removed to the Exchequer House in Edinburgh, and since this house connected with that of Bothwell, it is almost certain that for the first and only time in her life Mary broke her marriage vows. She was often callous, often flighty, but only in this case can she be charged with having been immoral. Living in the midst of such perils, it is only natural that she could not refuse herself to Bothwell; to lose him would have been too serious.

And Bothwell compassed the tragedy. He wanted to be rid of Darnley, so that he might marry Mary; the Queen saw Darnley as nothing but a danger; his fellow-conspirators could not forgive him for having betrayed them, after they had with his agreement assassinated Rizzio. Even then Mary did not connive clearly at the murder of Darnley, but, and here is weakness rather than crime, though she did not take part in the murder of her husband, she called him to Edinburgh, where he would live in the midst of dangers.

She loved Bothwell with a curious kind of madness, constantly reproaching him because he loved her not enough, with a strange abasement, as if she, the proud and ambitious Queen, desired to feel upon her neck the tread of his victorious foot. Lord Mar, who throughout had been her friend, she deposed from his rank as Keeper of Edinburgh Castle, to replace him by one of the flatterers of Bothwell. She gave her lover the castle of Blackness; she made him Superior of Leith; she presented him with jewels, with the furs which had belonged to her mother, Mary de Guise—she even gave him the ceremonial garments of Darnley, her murdered husband.

And yet she was not sure of Bothwell; she was jealous of him; she feared his infidelity. Before her marriage she hated Lady Bothwell, because this woman —unloved it is true—had a legitimate right to the use of the beloved name. This appears clearly in a sonnet Mary wrote in English :

> She for her honour's sake obeyeth you—
> I, obeying you, my dishonour seek.
> No wife, alas ! am I, as she to you ;
> Yet shall she not excel me, e'en in this.
> Constant she be, for profit to herself,
> For great her honour is to rule your state,
> Whilst my dear love with scorn alone be paid ;
> Yet shall she pass me not in duty leal.
> Tranquil she sleeps and dreams not of your ill,
> Whilst I in torment toss, lest evil fall.
> She did enjoy you with her friends' consent ;
> I, in despite of mine, will love you still.
> And yet, dear heart ! my loyalty you doubt,
> And firm assurance bear that she be true.

Such feelings are natural enough ; inevitable, indeed, in a woman possessed by love ; and Mary loved well. Here is a rough translation of a sonnet which she wrote in French :

> My love doth grow, and greater shall it grow,
> So long that I may live and to greatness shall cleave.
> Only that in his heart I may deserve a share,
> So that at last my love to him may manifest
> That never shall he find it opportune to doubt me.
> For him I love, all greatness I shall seek,
> And shall comport me so that he shall lastly see
> That I can find no joy, no pleasure, no content
> Save in obeying him, yea, in my loyal service.

It is for him alone that fortune I desire;
It is for him alone that health and life I need;
It is for him alone that virtue I would follow,
And all this life for him unchanged I will remain.

Even though a translation cannot render the grace of the French lines, it can render their abandonment. Mary was humbled indeed, for she had been conquered by the first strong man who appeared before her. One perceives this fact in another sonnet, where she suggests what is probably true—that Bothwell first prevailed over her by force. Again the present writer translates from the French:

It is for him that all my tears flow,
For him, the first who this weak form possessed,
Though not yet had he made my heart a slave,
Yet hard is the alarm which he afforded me
When of his blood in war he freely gave.
In this grief did he leave me, in my anguish,
Wherein my life I thought to lose, a-fearing
Thus to forgo the one rampart that arms me.
For him since then all honour I've despised,
A deed which can alone our happiness provide,
For him my conscience, my noble rank I hazard;
For him my friends forgone, my kindred all forgot,
And all other respects I contemplate as nothings:
Briefly, in you alone, my love, I seek my peace.

When one reads these sonnets, where so much love crosses the thread of so much misfortune, one is minded to pity Mary—not to blame her. One recalls the retort of the aged man in the "Republic" of Plato, who, condoled with because he was too old to

Robert Herdman

THE ABDICATION OF MARY QUEEN OF SCOTS

enjoy the pleasure of love, replied that he did not repine, since age had deprived him of a fierce and relentless enemy. Indeed, Mary was to be devoured without mercy by the rose-garlanded god that knows not pity.

But the marriage of Bothwell, though it rallied followers, at the same time raised once again factions among the nobles. A group of these proclaimed their loyalty to Mary Stuart, in the belief that she had been forced into marriage with Bothwell. Indeed, he had abducted her to Dunbar, just as we have shown that at the Exchequer House he forced his attentions upon her. But here intervene the long and difficult documents called the Casket Letters, the genuineness of which is not absolutely proved, but which seem to show that she wanted Bothwell, that she knew that she was to be abducted; that, in other words, she connived. And how easy it is to penetrate into this psychology!

Mary had suffered so much from men, had by her alliances caused the pouring out of so much blood, that she was now afraid to take any step. Therefore, she hoped that someone would be strong enough to take the step for her. If a strong man wished to abduct her, then let him abduct her, let him take the decision for her, and let her at last be at ease, holding to his strong arm.

Though Bothwell was strong, the feeling against Mary was stronger. All through the Protestant masses, as well as among the Protestant nobles, the epithets "adulteress," "murderess," "Jezebel," were applied to Mary, and a rising of the nobles took place against her chaotic and sanguinary government. Hurriedly, Bothwell mustered some forces, but swiftly at Carberry Hill came the encounter and the defeat. This was to Mary a tragic moment in her life, for before her surrender to the nobles she was forced to part from Bothwell. The man who had been a friend and a lover—coarse and brutal, it is true, but well-meaning enough—held her for a moment in his arms and rode away to Dunbar. She never saw him again. Mary was led to Edinburgh by her captors, while the people lined the roads, hurling at her biblical epithets.

Then the story takes a rapid turn. The Casket Letters suggested not very clearly, but quite clearly enough for sixteenth-century justice, that Mary had connived at the murder of Darnley; she might be charged with this crime; she might be burnt alive at the stake. A prisoner in the hands of the nobles, who were rid at last of a dominant sovereign, all she could do was to accept their terms: to resign her throne and allow her child to be crowned. All this she did, and she was imprisoned at Lochleven. After this the story of Mary is no longer a love-story. She goes from prison to prison. She escapes, for she still has a few partisans; but the Regent Moray is ready with a sufficient army, and Mary is defeated, flees across the border to throw herself upon the protection of Elizabeth.

One easily realises to what a state of despair Mary must have been driven before she craved mercy from Elizabeth. When Napoleon came on board the *Bellerophon* to seek asylum among his English enemies he was in safety, a man among men, a fallen political figure; but Mary, in the hands of Elizabeth, was a beautiful woman delivered to an ugly one, a cousin to a cousin, a claimant to the throne to the woman in possession. Elizabeth did not hesitate, for here at last was what she had worked for so many years: the possession of the body of Mary, Queen of Scots. She sent her from prison to prison, sometimes well treated, sometimes ill. In fact, Elizabeth, rejoicing in her triumph over Mary, insulted her by sending her a parcel containing two torn shirts, two pairs of worn shoes, and two pieces of velvet.

So the years passed, while Mary in prison wrote poetry, played music, and fascinated men. She fascinated even her gaolers, while Elizabeth kept her in prison, seeking the triumph of her policy. She wanted Mary to submit herself to judgment, so that the Darnley murder might be investigated by a court of law. If Mary were found not guilty, Elizabeth would restore her on the Scottish throne, provided that Mary abandoned her claim to that of England, that she abandoned her alliance with the French—and that she joined the Church of England. And by years of imprisonment, by years of loneliness, by her helplessness, Mary was overcome and accepted an Anglican chaplain.

Mary was taken to Sheffield Castle, where Lady Shrewsbury accused her of fascinating the Earl, but Elizabeth began to realise that the existence of Mary was a source of plots. A Catholic queen, imperfectly Protestant, provided a natural centre in England for Catholic plots against Elizabeth. Among these was the Ridolfi plot, which Elizabeth defeated. A rebellion arose in Scotland against the Regent, and Elizabeth watched with satisfaction the enfeeblement of Scotland, while she held Mary. There were other plots, for Mary radiated a legend of beauty and grace: the Throckmorton plot was stamped out; Mary's plot with the French to land troops and restore Catholicism was also exposed. Elizabeth was watchful, and every plot led to the death of those who joined in it.

Finally, Mary was involved in the Babington plot, the object of which was to assassinate Elizabeth and to bring in foreign Catholic troops. But this plot was discovered, and Babington, with six fellow-conspirators, suffered hanging at Tyburn. Babington, who had come near Mary Stuart, went to his death as Chastelard had gone to his death, as Rizzio had been assassinated, as Darnley had fallen under the murderer's knife. The aura of blood and disaster which spread about Mary's head involved all those who conspired for her sake or for her ideals. Until then Elizabeth had spared her, holding her as a useful hostage; but, realising that Mary was an inspiration to plots, she brought her to trial, made against her charges of treason which, in fact, were charges that she lived to the royal danger. She was sentenced to death.

And so, at the age of forty-four, Mary Stuart knelt before the block to make an end of a life which had brought nothing but disaster, and yet had created an immortal romance. Like Marie Antoinette, she died as well as she had lived ill. At the block she had the courage to remark to the executioner, who approached to remove her bodice, that she was not accustomed to such a waiting-maid. She prayed, knelt before the block, and three strokes severed her head from her body.

Thus died Mary Stuart, a woman who was not evil, but a woman who was vain. Too easily she aroused love, and she paid the penalty of beauty. Because of her loneliness and of her rank, men desired her, and desired her triumph. Being human, she was glad of her power of beauty as well as of her power of rank. Thus she encouraged that which destroyed her, and she destroyed as she was herself destroyed.

BIBLIOGRAPHY

Life of Mary, Queen of Scots, by Agnes Strickland (2 vols.).

The Fall of Mary Stuart, by F. A. Mumby.

The Tragedy of Mary Stuart, by Henry Shelley.

The Love Affairs of Mary, Queen of Scots, by Martin Hume.

Mary, Queen of Scots, by Elizabeth O'Neill. ("The People's Books.")

Mary, Queen of Scots: Her Tragedy and Environment, by T. F. Henderson (2 vols.).

The Mystery of Mary Stuart, by Andrew Lang.

BALZAC AND MADAME DE HANSKA

1.

VI. BALZAC AND MDME. DE HANSKA

THE FAITHFUL HEART

THE story of Honoré de Balzac and Madame de Hanska can be summarised in a single tragic sentence: he loved her for seventeen years and enjoyed matrimony for five months. It seems that what the Greeks would have called Fate had made up a long account against one of the greatest French writers, perhaps a writer for all time. Though Balzac enjoyed much reputation, many of the satisfactions to vanity that all men desire, though he did encounter the one great human joy—namely true and constant love—his life is one of misery and of stress. He was gifted, but he paid for his gifts.

Honoré de Balzac was born in 1799, and died in 1850. Those fifty-one years were fuller, more ardent, than any wise man would desire. He was born in misfortune, and died in tardy happiness, perhaps not even in happiness, but merely in one of those fulfilments of desire rather akin to the pension which a broken man receives at sixty-five, after having the whole of his life denied himself all joys. He held Madame de Hanska, held his dream, but no better perhaps than a man who carries in his hands a butterfly that seeks an outlet between his fingers.

Honoré was certainly ill-favoured by birth, for his father—a curious person, in some ways akin to his great son—had before his marriage taken one of those drastic courses which recall Honoré. Balzac Senior, as he approached fifty, made up his mind that he would never marry, and invested the whole of his capital so that it might bring him in an annuity, after which it would revert to the corporation which paid him his income. A few years later he married a young and attractive woman, who brought him very little property, and endowed him with four children. Since the annuity was punctually paid Honoré could be brought up in comfort, but he could hope for no inheritance. He was, therefore, worse off than the son of poor parents, because he was being given comfort instead of hard conditions. He was being unfitted for the struggle for life, and yet promised nothing to make the struggle easy.

He was the victim of a very common state of things: his mother did not love him, because she was of the type which cares for babies; as Honoré was followed by his brothers and sisters, his mother's affection was shifted from him to the youngest, as a result of which he was deported from his home, placed with a foster-mother, with whom he remained for four years, seeing little of his parents. Thus he did not know love in his early days, and he was not to know it later, for as he passed from childhood into boyhood his mother, evidently determined to be rid of him, placed him at the Oratorian School at Vendôme, an amazing school akin to a prison, a school recalling Dotheboys Hall. For six years Balzac remained in this school without ever emerging from it for a holiday, a Sunday, or even half a day.

It was part of the Oratorian principle to take over a child entirely, body and soul. What this did for Balzac's soul is undefined, since he never was numbered among the fervent; as regards his body, finding it irritable, speculative, and wilful, the masters abundantly punished it by locking it up in a cell six feet each way, a cell where no light penetrated; they castigated this body with wooden ferules; to tame it completely they often fed it upon bread and water. The terrible story is to be found in one of Balzac's early novels, *Louis Lambert*.

Finally, when this regime proved too effective, Balzac became ill, so ill that he was withdrawn and taken home, where he arrived like a creature escaping from gaol, not daring to say what he thought lest he be punished, not daring to have an opinion, shrinking away from his own shadow. However, his mind was too active, his intelligence too sharp, to allow of a mental breakdown. Though his constitution was wrecked, and though six years at school had taken twenty years from his life, liberty and the affection of his father, together with the tolerance of his mother, by degrees developed him. We find him reading persistently, attending classes, passing from boyhood into adolescence; he was then rather a plump youth of middle size, with extremely dark eyes, dark hair, and a pugnacious appearance. The nose is so aggressive, the chin so pronounced, the gaze so dark and brooding, that one half understands why his masters at Vendôme locked him up in a dark cell. How else could they have controlled him?

Meanwhile, he was forming his character and

developing through the influence of his tutor, Lepitre, the Royalist views which he held all through his life. It may seem rather peculiar that Balzac, the man who saw so clearly the mechanism of commerce and of politics, should have been a fervent Royalist in the France of Louis XVIII. It would have been more natural for him to join the Republicans, even though Lepitre moulded him into a Legitimist shape. But Balzac was held away from the Republican side because he was a snob. His name was not *de* Balzac, but merely Balzac. Yet he held for royalty and the aristocracy a worship so slavish that he made more or less affected researches into archives, from which he came out waving the valuable "de" like a fox-terrier that has found a bone. His novels are infected by this snobbery. He believes in the aristocratic type; he is attracted mainly to women of noble birth. In other words, he is a typical specimen of the reaction from the French Revolution.

In those days, a few years after the fall of Napoleon—that last product of the French Revolution, that triumph of democracy—Europe was under the sway of the Holy Alliance, an alliance designed to maintain kingship and the practice of the true faith. It found supporters because Europe was weary after twenty-five years of war, international and civil. The virtues were out of date, because the French revolutionaries had exaggerated purity, loyalty, public spirit. The period reverted to the eighteenth century, to powder for faces and purchase for reputations. Scepticism and free thought were out of date, because the revolution had worshipped the god of reason. The world was

HONORÉ DE BALZAC

tired, as much enfeebled by loss of blood and by empty treasuries as the world of 1919.

It is not remarkable, therefore, that Balzac should have expressed that spirit, because a man is great only in so far as he expresses his period. All this will appear when we come to consider the quality of the love which Balzac bore Madame de Hanska.

Since, however, he did not discover his Dulcinea until he reached the age of thirty-one, we must say something of his start in literature, and indicate the course of his life, because this was powerfully to influence his relations with his beloved. Naturally, he was not destined for literature; no respectable family, such as the Balzacs, could have destined a son to write novels, any more than they could have destined Joan of Arc for visions.

He was placed in a lawyer's office, where he was kindly treated and acutely miserable, because he detested the practice of the law. Mentally he was interested, and in reading his novels it is clear that his grasp of legal procedure was close and profound, but he was æsthetically unhappy. The law dealt only with actualities, and afforded no outlet to the imagination that soared in him. In the lawyer's office he was akin to one of those tragic eagles who fix resigned eyes upon a blue sky glimpsed through bars. He worked, he read, and there formed in him a decision which, before he was twenty, made him unmanageable: he did not want to be a lawyer, he wanted to write.

His father, kind to all his children, was willing enough to give him his way, but his mother, who appears throughout his life as an evil genius, strove for a long time against her son's desires. In fact, Madame Balzac was not cruel, but she was hard. Her conception of life for her children was obedience, order, and thrift. Any revolt against these three qualities was sinful; since sin was hateful, it was a mother's duty to repress it; therefore, she must instil the three virtues by force. How one understands that type of mind, as hard to itself as to other people! How one realises Madame Balzac, hard-working, faithful, loyal to her husband, industrious on behalf of her children, wholly virtuous, and destined to make misery. However, her son was too strong for her, and her husband was too weak to support her. Also, Balzac was encouraged by his sister Laure, who proved his most intimate friend throughout his life.

Thus Balzac is allowed to stay at home; then to move to a garret of his own, where he can write. And here one perceives the action of Madame Balzac, for she placed her son in this garret, providing him only with a bed, a table, and two chairs. She gave him an allowance so small that he would certainly have starved if a kind old woman had not helped him. He could not afford a fire, and we find him writing to his sister, begging her to send him a coverlet and an old shawl. He has colds, he had toothache, and yet he aspires to buy a piano. Pathetic Balzac! The garret is too small for a piano. It is characteristic of him that throughout his life the schemes will be too large for the garret.

Thus, in circumstances of the most intense discomfort, he composed a play, *Cromwell*, which was a failure and deserved to so be, also a number of novels, left unfinished. The failure of *Cromwell* was so obvious that it could not be played, and that his family, weary of maintaining him in the garret in Paris, insisted on his return to their house at Villeparisis. He was beaten, and for five years, confined within a family circle that became hostile when his sister Laure left home to marry, he composed a number of romantic novels, as was the fashion in those days—novels devoid of much importance, and interesting only the *amateurs* of Balzac. His earnings did not seem to promise future independence; for one book he obtained eight hundred francs, for another thirteen hundred and twenty-five. In three years he composed thirty-one volumes, working then, as he was to work throughout his life, fifteen hours in every day.

Not because he revolted against work, but because he was one of those optimistic, excitable men who seek short cuts to fortune, at the age of twenty-five he managed to place himself in a position which was to hold him down until he died. He found a sympathetic friend to assist him, opened a publishing business for the issue of classical works. He obtained enough money for rent and for production, but he had forgotten advertisement. He could not sell his books; by the end of the year had lost fifteen thousand francs. It was disaster, and his stock was sold for the value of paper.

If his spirit had not been so high it would have been better for him, but Balzac, determined to start once more, obtained thirty thousand francs from his father and headed further towards ruin. He had to pay fifteen thousand francs for a printing licence, fifteen thousand francs for materials, and twelve thousand francs to his partner. He started with a working capital that was represented only by debts. If he had striven to progress slowly, the situation might yet have been saved, but Balzac, inflamed by his schemes, purchased a type foundry; the new expenses weighed down the already overloaded business. In a general crash the enterprise closed down, the type foundry was sold, and Balzac, aged twenty-eight, started in life with debts some forty times larger than his annual earnings.

That is the keynote of Balzac, debt, and it is debt which all through his correspondence with Laure, with Madame de Hanska, with his friend, Madame de Bernys, mingles with plans of novels, keen pictures of men and women, and extravagant ideas. Balzac was to blame, but Balzac would not have been himself if he had had another temperament.

We have no space in the present essay to give a full statement of the books of Balzac, but it is essential to say something of the work of so remarkable a man. We may exclude works like *Louis Lambert* and *La Peau de Chagrin*, because these are mainly biography. Though Balzac made one of his first successes with *La Physiologie du Mariage*, merely because it was thought to be shocking in that virtuous Victorian century, he will survive, if he survives, by two groups of novels, falling within the classification of Scenes of Private Life and Scenes of Public Life. The two together compose what he called *La Comédie Humaine*, a bitter, gibing comedy. It is not likely that he conceived together the whole series of novels, but his attention was drawn now to provincial life, then to political life, then to the army, until, by degrees, he found himself covering the whole of the human field.

The most notable of his novels are probably *Le Père Goriot*, *Eugénie Grandet*, and *La Cousine Bette*. Here we find Balzac's immense knowledge of provincial life, where the days trickle one by one, imperceptibly sowing white hair upon the heads and growing moss upon the stones. We find a simple, always human vision of the life of ordinary people, who are born, who marry, who die, who make foolish sacrifices, who inherit money and enjoy it, who harbour vanity, who are seldom faithless, ignoble, or heroic—who are merely commonplace people. In *Le Père Goriot* we find the tragedy of a new King Lear, living in an abominable boarding-house where food is weighed and laundry hesitated over, while rich daughters leave the old man to die in ignominy. There we find the last of the romantic characters, Vantrin, the inspired rogue, through whose ravings we see life as Balzac saw it at the end of a fifteen-hour day, sustained by a jugful of black coffee.

In other novels, in the novels of Paris, we see the other side of Balzac, the lustful side, the mad side—namely the invasion of Paris, the conquest of wealth by the adventurers from the provinces, as the railways came, as industry developed, as wealth began to sprout. Zola, coming later, exhibited the mad race for wealth better than Balzac, in books called *La Curée* and *L'Argent*, because he had more details before him, but no one better than Balzac could create a character like Lucien de Rubempre, the adventurer, or

Rastignac, another of those who depend only upon their wits and upon their ruthlessness.

The eighteen-forties in France, in England, in America, were years of financial and industrial development. Balzac, first from his garret, later at Les Jardies—a small house near Paris—had enough social contacts, and, above all, enough imagination, to realise and to paint the bubbling pot of politics and cash where swirled men, women, bank-accounts, and thrones.

And he worked, in the most terrible, in the most tragic way. He spent approximately fifteen hours a day at his desk, in bouts of three or four hours, sustained by four or five hours' sleep. When he flagged he stimulated himself with black coffee, and, being conscientious, he produced his work as painfully as a man may. As soon as his manuscript was composed he sent it to the printer. When the proofs returned to the printer some two-thirds had been cut out, re-written, written in the margins, scribbled on the back; the manuscript had perhaps been crumpled into a ball because Balzac despaired of it. A new proof would arrive, and once again this would be scribbled over; it would be cut in two, and pages of manuscript would be inserted. Then it would be cut up again, stuck upon fragments of newspaper. We have a vision of Balzac perspiring in a hot room, worn out, his stomach turning against the coffee, cutting, adding, half in tears, half in exaltation, perhaps without food, dressed in dirty old clothes, without a collar, composing in a sort of fury.

Such a man was doomed to failure, because success

comes most easily to those who work easily. If he had not laboured so much, if he had not been fit to compose each year six or seven novels and plays, together with hundreds of articles and short stories, committing here and there a page which is classical, he would certainly have starved. And this for three reasons. The first was the chaos in which he worked; the second his indebtedness; the third his mania for schemes leading to fortune.

The results of the chaos are obvious enough. When a writer continually recomposes his work, when he fails to deliver on the due date, he quarrels with his editors and publishers. Balzac had many; his fame, which increased slowly, forced the magazines to deal with him, but he maddened them. A serial was begun and left unfinished; in one case he did not finish at all a story which had begun to appear, so that the editor rightly blamed him for infuriating his readers. Continually, money was advanced to him, after which he declared himself unable to deliver the manuscript, and this was added to his debts. Or he would grow tired, take back his work, and make himself liable for payment therefor.

As for the schemes and the extravagances, they enlighten us still more on the disaster of his life. When he acquired a country place for which he could not pay, he conceived the absurd idea of erecting gigantic greenhouses which would capture the sun. There he would grow thousands of pineapples to supply the Paris market. He would make a hundred thousand francs a year, four hundred thousand francs. The greenhouses were never built; but in later years

Balzac spent much time and money on investigating lead- and silver-mines in Sardinia. He always had hope, though he had not money. He wished to enter Parliament; he was three times a candidate to the Académie Française. He thought himself capable of leading a political life, a social life, a literary life, and a commercial life. He took no exercise, he played no games, and in a sense he had no loves, save his ideal love for the distant Madame de Hanska. Our vision of Balzac must be that of some sort of radio-active material, which is in intense internal movement, giving off emanations and destroying itself as it produces.

He had friends, and several women inspired his life. The first was Madame de Bernys, twenty-two years his senior, who gave him the affection which his mother had refused to him. There was the Duchesse d'Abrantes; and there was Madame de Castries, one of those queer worldlings who take up lions. She possibly accepted Balzac as a lover, then suddenly discarded him because she was tired of him, because she knew him well enough, because she had achieved him. There was Madame Visconti, with whom he travelled. Above all, there was Madame de Hanska. Several friends liked and appreciated him—George Sand, Victor Hugo, Théophile Gautier—the greatest of his period. But Madame de Hanska alone mattered to him in the profound sense, and now that we approach the recital of the seventeen years which he gave to this woman we are able to appreciate his anguished life. In his letters to this lady he describes his existence as it is, and the tragedy of it is immense. He is so poor, so laden with debt, that sometimes he does not write to her because he cannot meet the postal charges on the letter.

Madame de Hanska appears in the life of Balzac in 1830. She appears in the way which would seem least well-designed to attract a man of dominating talent: she writes to him that she has read some of his novels, that, lost in her castle in Ukraine, his thought brings to her the rumble of the great world, and understanding of life. At least we may assume this, since the letter was burnt with the rest of her correspondence some seventeen years later. Since Balzac received many letters from admirers, notably from women, some of whom made amorous proposals, we must believe that the letter was charming. Balzac was so indifferent to this sort of correspondence that in many cases his answers were written by his sister, by Madame de Bernys, by any person who happened to be near. Perhaps—one hardly likes to say it, but it may be so—Balzac was pleased because the lady was the wife of M. *de* Hanski, a great nobleman with a castle in Ukraine. Barbey d'Aurevilly once led along the boulevards a lobster tied to a ribbon; Balzac was inclined to give his heart exercise in the more fashionable world.

Such remarks may seem unfair, but we may not pretend that Balzac's love was entirely selfless, entirely humble; deep and enduring as it was, it contained the human alloy of vanity which perhaps makes love strong. In that sense Madame de Hanska was a suitable object for the emotions of a poor and unhappy man. Eva Hanska belonged to an historic Polish family, and was born in 1805. Very young, she married M. de Hanski, twenty-five years her senior, kind enough, though rather stupid, who gave her five children, of whom four died, leaving only Countess Anna, to whom she so devoted herself that much trouble came to Balzac. She was an attractive woman, with a dark complexion, dark hair, and rather full, imperious lips. She had very dark, soft eyes, and was beautifully shaped, having the most delightful hands, and sloping shoulders. She was intelligent, speaking several languages, and having a taste for literature. She lived in a Russia that was still barbarous, a Russia upon which the innovations of Peter the Great had made little impression; Ukraine was not far from the Cossack country.

One may easily imagine that this woman of refinement and culture, imprisoned in a wilderness such as may now be discovered in the backwoods of Brazil, not only took pleasure in the literature of cultivated France, but also sought an outlet for her ideas by writing to the authors whom she admired. One suspects that Madame Hanska wrote to other authors, possibly to Jules Sandeau, to George Sand, to Gautier. But they were not so ambitious as Balzac, and she lived a long way off.

Whatever may be the situation, the correspondence begins in 1830, and ends only in 1849, when the two marry. Balzac's letters have been collected under the title *Lettres à l'étrangère*, and are more interesting than any other collection of love-letters, because Balzac treats Madame Hanska like a wife; he does not merely protest his love, but he states his plans, the sales of his work; he discusses his troubles, his finances, his lawsuits, schemes, and disappointments. Nothing could be more touching than this complete self-exposure of a great man to the eyes of a woman who is interested but who does not love. We may quote from among these letters to give an idea of the quality of the relationship.

For instance, early in 1833, when he is in love, yet dares not say so, he says that he has invested Madame Hanska with the three main qualities of her nation, with the love of poetry, of music, and of God. He says that in his gaze she would recognise the gratitude of the lover and the religion of the friend, the pure tenderness which binds the son to his mother, the brother to his sister, and all the respect for a woman that a young man may have. At last—and this is pathetic—he begs her to separate in her mind the author from the man; he hints at his poverty, his loneliness; he casts himself at her feet, and it is not wonderful that she tramples him. A little later he reveals himself openly.

"I love you, sweet Unknown, and this strange thing is the natural fact in a life always empty and wretched, which I have filled only with ideas, and whose agonies I have reduced only by the pleasures of fantasy."

What a terrible phrase! What flowers to fasten to love's garland! And always he complains that he has no time to devote himself to her as he would—to her, the distant and radiant phantom. He sends her his books, begs her opinion of them, and receives it with a strange mixture of arrogance and humility. He complains: "Out of low envy the editor of the

Revue de Paris holds back for a week my third article. . . . These people bargain for me as for an ornament; at one moment I experience their malice; then anonymous insults in the album of the *Revue*; or they lie servile at my feet. When 'Marana' came out they printed that I was mad."

By degrees the correspondence exasperates him. He wants to see her. She has described herself to him and he has her picture, but he needs fuller satisfaction, and writes to her:

"You, you, my dear star, you fear to see me, you are young and beautiful; you load me with unfair suspicions. Those who have suffered never betray; it is they who are betrayed."

He is love-mad. In the same letter he writes:

"To-morrow if she wished it I should break my pen; to-morrow no other woman should hear my voice."

And in this letter comes an extremity of pathos, because, though he is willing to speak to no woman if Madame Hanska so wishes, he begs that she may not part him from Madame de Bernys, aged fifty-eight, and to him another mother. He begs her, she so young, not to be jealous of his old friend.

But Madame Hanska is hard; she does not love the man, but he interests her intensely, and perhaps she would more easily bear the young washerwoman who made a quarrel between George Sand and Sandeau than the fact of Madame de Bernys, for that woman holds something of Balzac's mind, and that is what Madame Hanska loves. Fortunately Madame de Bernys died before Madame Hanska could persuade

Balzac to expel her from his regard. Indeed, he was mad for her when he had not seen her, and their first meeting at Neufchâtel increased his madness :

> "My God, how beautiful you were on Sunday, in your violet frock ! How you have smitten my fancy ! . . . My adored flower, I fear from you all that jealousy inspires . . . my adored one, my wife. Know that whatever I may write you, when I am driven by labour, unhappy or joyous, in my soul lives an immense love ; you fill my heart, you fill my life ; though I cannot always express this love, nothing shall alter it ; always shall it bloom again more beautiful, newer, more gracious, because it is true love, because true love ever increases. True love is a beautiful perennial flower planted in the heart, which spreads its leaves and its branches, which every season increases its fruits and strengthens its perfumes ; so, my dear life, tell me, repeat me always, that nothing shall hurt its bark, its delicate leaves, that always it shall grow in our two hearts, beloved, as a life within our lives, a single life ! Oh, how I love you ! Ah, such balm does this love spread about me that pain seems impossible. You see, you are my strength."

And he promises that in times to come they shall make Neufchâtel the object of love's pilgrimage. At one point that most tragic of all letters appears : Balzac has not written to his beloved because he had not the money with which to frank the letter. So one wonders what impression these letters can have made upon the noble and idle lady. She cannot have understood what it meant to work fifteen hours a day, to lack money, to be pursued by creditors. These things did not happen in her world. She could not have grasped why Balzac should suddenly tire of a novel, withdraw it from the hands of Girardin, and involve himself into yet more thousands of francs of debt. All that struggle was remote. Perhaps, in fact, that was one of the attractions of Balzac; he was to her a Bohemian, and she might not have believed in his genius if he had driven from the Champs Élysées in a well-furnished barouche.

However, Balzac drew her and held her, though they met so seldom. Their first meeting took place at Neufchâtel, where Balzac travelled to greet her and M. de Hanski. They met alone for the first time on the Promenade du Faubourg; they were alone under a great tree in the Val de Travers, where they declared love and swore to wait for each other. For they were clean people, and there was no suggestion of a furtive intrigue. Madame Hanska was married, and, since her husband was so greatly her senior, she could expect ultimate widowhood. Then she would marry Balzac, become the wife of the greatest living literary figure, honourably and openly. Whether M. de Hanski knew that some relationship existed between the two is not certain, but it is likely, and it seems that he tolerated it, because he was so vain that the friendship of Balzac was precious to him. (Here, no doubt, the reader recalls the attitude of Sir William Hamilton in regard to his wife and to Nelson.)

The correspondence continues, Balzac always finding

new words to paint his passion, and always he describes his fears, his troubles. To Madame Hanska he must have represented the uncertain side of life, the life where something happens materially, and not merely in the spirit. Perhaps she even enjoyed his disasters, because they were dramatic. We find in the correspondence a better outline of Balzac's life than we could find in a diary, because he makes an effort to express himself to his beloved. He outlines a career that is constantly heart-rending. A fire breaks out at the printing-office and destroys a large portion of *Contes Drolatiques*; he loses three thousand five hundred francs, and fails to receive six thousand.

He cannot live without Madame Hanska, and so he takes a post-carriage for the whole journey from Paris, which costs him fifteen thousand francs. He raises this no one knows how, perhaps from moneylenders, perhaps by selling at any price work which should have fetched three or four times more, perhaps by mortgaging his future energy to gain advances. Even so he has at Vienna a pathetic quarrel with Madame Hanska, because there he insists upon working twelve hours a day, while he explains to her that he is making a great concession to his love for her that he steals for her sake three hours out of every day. The reader must not say that he did not love Madame Hanska, and that he loved his work more. That is not true, but work had become a force so dominating that even when, for a few days, he found himself in her radiance, he could no more forbear from writing than from eating. Perhaps she would have loved him more if she had dominated his work: the conquest of his heart was not enough.

Time passes; Balzac lives foolishly, Orientally; riddled with debts, he takes a box at the opera and decorates his table with rare flowers. He who had been so slovenly for a while becomes a dandy, and makes Paris talk about his priceless walking-stick. Terrible things happen to him: his uncorrected proofs are sold by an unscrupulous editor, and appear, of all painful places, in St. Petersburg, and in Russian. A lawsuit followed, in which Balzac was described as immoral and dishonest. And though Balzac won the case, it was not decided whether the uncorrected proofs should be handed back. He became ill. He had been ill before; now he lost Madame de Bernys, and could not replace her by a new friend, Madame Marbouty. Time passes, troubles accumulate; his publisher fails, and Balzac, who had signed bills for him, is involved to the extent of thirteen thousand francs.

Then comes the mad journey to Sardinia to develop silver- and lead-mines, a journey which piles up more debt; he purchases Les Jardies, loading upon his back still more debt. He had neuralgia, and yet, still bubbling with enterprise, he created the *Revue Parisienne*, which broke after three months. Balzac trusted so much in his energy and his capacity for work that he was always willing to contract a new debt or to enter into a new venture; he might owe money, but those terrible days and nights of work would meet the deficit. All through, his love for Madame Hanska, their very rare meetings, served like a torch to light his path. But the twelve years of the early correspondence were gay and happy compared with the seven which were to follow. In 1842 M. de Hanski died, and Balzac, aged forty-three, saw before him a promise of fulfilment. Wretched Balzac! Seven years were laboured for Leah, and seventeen for Madame Hanska.

He did not at first understand that he was not to have his desire at once; he was surprised because she would not let him come to her, though she had not seen him for seven years. Only by degrees did he realise that to call upon so recent a widow would be a breach of good manners. Her empire was so absolute that he waited eighteen months before venturing on this gross infraction of the rules of good society. He was happy then, for he felt sure of her, and, besides, life was more promising, in spite of a disaster following upon his play, *Les Ressources de Quinola*. At last, in that year of release, the *Comédie Humaine* was collected, and he was hailed, if not as a popular man, at least a great man. Only Madame Hanska did he need to make the time such as Faust desired:

> When I shall say to the fleeting moment,
> "Tarry awhile, thou art so sweet."

Madame Hanska was reaching middle age, but he loved her still, but though she maintained with him her correspondence, and though they were practically betrothed, there was no definite talk of marriage.

Here we should say something of Madame Hanska's side. Being a lady of quality and the heir to a large estate, she was a ward of the Tsar; his consent to her marriage with a foreigner would certainly be refused, unless she resigned to her daughter the whole of her property. Now, had her affections turned towards a foreigner who was wealthy, or even reasonably secure, she would probably have married him without the consent of the Tsar. But when we reflect on the conditions which Balzac had exhibited to her for a dozen years—of the poverty, the lawsuits, the debts—we cannot blame Madame Hanska for having paused and asked herself whether she was willing to harness to her matrimonial chariot a creature so wild. She did not immeasurably love Balzac, or she would have risked everything, but she loved him well, and it must not be counted entirely against her that she had prudence, that she desired some sort of security—that the roof overhead would not be threatened by bailiffs, and that there would every day be food upon her plate.

We may believe, however, that one of the causes of delay was this : Madame Hanska was a mother before she was a wife, and her passion for her only surviving child, the Countess Anna, was such that at last she definitely refused to marry Balzac until the girl was married. This happened in 1846, four agonising years after the death of M. de Hanski. Balzac went east, the Hanska family came west. They met more often, and the engagement was made definite ; but even so, even after the marriage of Anna, Madame Hanska hesitated a further three years. One may wish that we had the letters of those last years ; one would certainly observe there a mixture of fear of poverty and of weariness. She had been bound to Balzac so long that she saw no reason why the bond should be made more definite. She was reaching middle age ;

why not go peacefully towards the end in security, in comfort, and in mutual companionship?

But Balzac would not have it. He was snatched up. He was mad. Even his work is affected. At last Madame Hanska is obtaining her desire, and causing him to fail again and again at his new novel. In fact, because she bade him meet her at Dresden, he interrupted his work completely, leaving a contract in the middle of its execution. And yet he is unhappy, ill, neuralgic; now his heart was affected. He says: "Nothing amuses me, nothing distracts me, nothing animates me." He quarrels with Madame Hanska, who charges him with proclaiming too openly his passion for her.

At last as time passes, as Madame Hanska becomes kinder, he prepares the dwelling where she will live, in the Rue Fortunée, a dwelling more sumptuous than he can afford, binding himself to more debt, quarrelling with his mother, who does not like Madame Hanska, who does not wish to acquire for him a possibly penniless bride. Chaos, still chaos, and still waiting, until at last comes the year 1849, when Balzac approaches his desire, but like a spent runner winning a race, who falls fainting across the tape. He is very ill, he cannot face exertion, his heart weakens every day; and Madame Hanska is so cruel, so determined to assert her strength, that even now she threatens to break off her engagement. But perhaps she hesitated before a determination so severe after a relationship so long.

In March 1850, at Berditchef, Balzac and Madame Hanska were united. He took her home to Paris, took her into the asylum of his heart. And, as if an evil omen awaited them, the house was lit up and the rooms decked with flowers, but the couple could not gain admittance, because the valet had gone mad.

Five months did Balzac enjoy his wife, for he did enjoy her—cheerful, gay, and assured that this woman of forty-four was young and beautiful. With her by his side he could make a reputation greater than the one which he held. But though the mind was strong, the heart was weak, and the power of the emotions which he gained from his beloved did, in five months, damage which might have been spread over years. Perhaps, too, it was the pursuit of Madame Hanska maintained Balzac alive. He lived because he wanted her, and when he gained her he had nothing more to live for.

Thus comes a day in August 1850 when Balsac is dying, when Victor Hugo comes to see him for the last time, and says in a sarcastic tone that Madame Balzac was crying a great deal. It is Victor Hugo who tells us the story of the end. He entered the room where Balzac lay unconscious, watched by an old woman; Balzac's wife had gone to her room. An old woman, a nurse, and a servant stopped beside the bed, while Victor Hugo, for the last time, pressed Balzac's hand. Thus he died, while his wife wept in her apartments, and his aged mother alone stayed by his bedside.

After the death of Balzac, when the house fell into other hands, and its contents were scattered, so were the latest letters of Balzac to his beloved. They were found, some in a cobbler's shop, used for booking orders to re-sole shoes; some were found at a grocer's shop, about to wrap butter. They were scattered, torn up to make bills, turned into paper boats for small boys. The essence of Balzac's passion went down into the street, and at the corners of the houses the wind chased it right away.

BIBLIOGRAPHY

Honoré de Balzac, by Mary F. Sanders.

Lettres à l'étrangère.

Balzac, by Sir Frederick Wedmore. ("Great Writers" Series.)

Balzac, *Memoir*, by Wormeley.

Main Currents of Nineteenth-Century Literature, by George Brandes.

CATHERINE THE GREAT

VII. CATHERINE THE GREAT

CATHERINE, Empress of Russia, hardly deserves the title of "Great." When to the name of a sovereign we attach that word, we mean that notable achievements have marked the reign, that between the accession of the monarch and his death a great change has come over his country, and that he has shaped the destiny of his people.

To a certain extent Catherine the Great can claim to have affected Russia, because she was a warrior by temperament and set back her frontiers, but that is not much. The world has known many conquerors—Ghengis Khan, Tamburlane, the Mogul, the Roman Cæsar, Napoleon I—and the frontiers which they pushed across the map have been pushed back again. Conquest is nothing; consolidation is everything.

In that sense Catherine was not great. Napoleon has claims to greatness because he created institutions, national conscription, and tobacco monopoly, State theatres, and, above all, the first codified law. Frederick the Great deserves his title because he made Prussia out of a weak and disunited state; Bismarck is still greater because he formed Germany out of a chaos of little countries.

Henry the Navigator gave greatness to Portugal by creating its colonial empire. And Elizabeth of England placed her mark not only upon the tyranny of the seas, but upon British commercial organisation.

Every nation has had one great monarch; otherwise it would not now be a nation.

In that sense Catherine of Russia is not great. She was a great personality, but she was not a great sovereign. No woman could have lived a life so chaotic and so subservient to animal passion, yet have been a great sovereign. That is an achievement which men can sometimes compass, but women not; in queens purity, or comparative purity, is the basis of all power. It will at once be obvious that it is fair to call Catherine a creature of her period. Born in 1729, she lived till 1796, thus compassing most of the eighteenth century—that wonderful century of mental excitement, popular upheaval, cynicism, and nation building. Had she been born a hundred years earlier, her career would have been less exciting, because she would have been less influenced, and would have remained merely a barbaric sovereign. Had she been born a hundred years later, it is difficult to predict what this Russian compound with Victorianism would have achieved in the nineteenth century.

Catherine was not actually in the line of the Russian throne. She obtained it by marriage, by force—possibly by murder; she maintained herself in the same way. After the death of Peter the Great came a series of Russian sovereigns so contemptible that in contrast they endow Catherine II with virtue. Catherine I, Anne, Elizabeth—all these have left in history only a brilliant chaos. They occupied nearly fifty years in debauchery and in pageantry. Not a single achievement of lasting value came out of these people, out of these followers of Peter, a man who certainly deserved to be called great.

Peter was a strange incident in the Russian line. He was a man not content with making war upon Sweden, making war upon any neighbour, but determined—he a man of the seventeenth century—to modernise his country. It was an amazing country, almost entirely Eastern though Greek Orthodox in religion; it was in a sense the heir of the Eastern Roman Empire; the colour of Byzantium, its rule—half-pious, half-bloody—its engrossment in intrigue, a little of its polish, and all its savagery had filtered into Russia. Peter the Great—this early modern—strove to force these doors. He wanted to lead the West into Russia; he worked with his own hands in England to discover the art of shipbuilding; he brought into Russia the elements of industry, much to the anger and dismay of the peasant homes.

He found a Russia where men wore *caftans*—and he introduced them to Western dress. He insisted that they should cut off their beards. That sounds trifling, but the appearance of clean-shaven men, the destruction of the patriarchal air, had more effect upon Russia than would have had any measure short of compulsory education. The clean-shaven face was the West, while the beards were the old East.

The results, however, were not immediate. A clipped head does not necessarily develop brains. If the followers of Peter the Great had been of his temperament, Russia would have evolved at least a century earlier because they would have continued the work. Instead, they neglected the ordinances of

Peter; much of the population slipped back, while the Germans, and to a certain extent the French, arrived in Russia, bringing Western culture to a select group. As a result, the cleavage between the rich and the poor, which a century before had not been very notable, became profound. Not so much the nobility, but the official class began to segregate itself from the people. Hence jealousy and friction, hence tyranny, and hence, too, a situation which would have required, not so much a stronger personality than Catherine, but a better-ordered brain. She herself stated that in her policy she was guided by "circumstances, conjectures, and conjunctions"—in fact, she was guided by nothing at all, except the lover of the day or a fit of temper.

Catherine was born at Stettin, as Princess Sophie of Anhalt-Zerbst, daughter of a major-general in the Prussian Army, Prince Christian Augustus. To the brother of this prince the Empress Elizabeth had been betrothed, and no doubt there ran through her mind a certain sentimentality, which inclined her to his brother, and therefore to his niece. The young princess was as well educated as a girl could be in those days, for she had a natural curiosity, which showed itself all through her life. Without being essentially Western, she was infinitely more intelligent than any Russian contemporary. Therefore the sentiment of Elizabeth and the attainments of the princess worked together, so that when the princess attained fifteen she was summoned to the court of St. Petersburg to become the betrothed of her cousin, the Grand Duke Charles Peter, heir presumptive of the Russian throne.

Such a proposition was naturally immensely attractive

to a minor German prince, and the princess was sent to St. Petersburg with the blessing of her parents, who hoped through this alliance to achieve a great destiny. Thus the princess was betrothed to the young Grand Duke, who was only one year her senior, and adopted the name of Catherine. She also gave up the Lutheran religion and accepted the Greek Orthodox faith, in which she was educated by a Russian prelate.

It is known that Catherine made a good impression in St. Petersburg, for her upbringing did not at all correspond with the prevalent ideals of this court, but, though she was only fifteen, she determined to make herself fit for her destiny—to Russianise herself. She determined to learn Russian, to speak it well, which is always a difficult task; since she now belonged to the Greek Orthodox Church, she would know its laws and its practice. Thus we find the young princess withdrawing often from the revelry of the court to sit with her books and her masters. This made a good impression, probably because man always feels a little guilty when he confronts his pleasures. Catherine had another virtue, a certain sobriety, which pleased a people somewhat sated with the wildness and extravagance of Elizabeth's court. She was not beautiful, but pleasing.

The picture which lies before the present writer shows a rather plump girl (who was destined to be stout), dark hair thrown back from a fine, intelligent forehead, with which contrasts a distinctly foolish nose and mouth. In that face we find a hint of humour in the eyes, but for the rest, heaviness, dullness. One does not know in what circumstances this woman will be foolish and when she will be wise. One cannot discover sensuality in the features, but this, no doubt, would be excluded from a Court portrait.

Still, as she is, with these contrasts and with these charms, we find her at the court of Elizabeth. This empress, like her successor, was a simple personality. A *coup d'état* had given her possession of the Empress Anne and of the infant heir to the throne. She was dictator of Russia, but at first in an uncertain position. To hold the Russian throne was not an easy matter for a girl of eighteen, which she was at the time of her accession. But Elizabeth, though she was dissipated, was not foolish, and realised that the quickest way to power was through the support of the army. Nature had endowed her to receive this support, because she was a tall and stately woman, and because she had not the slightest sense of personal dignity. All her life she familiarised herself with the army by electing to her favours any handsome guardsman whom she admired. Rumour gives her love affairs with over three hundred men in the guard regiments. This may be exaggerated, but it indicates a state of looseness which had a natural effect upon the court. Hence the tone of the Russian court was a very low one. Catherine, with her inclinations towards learning and order, was, at the age of fifteen, precipitated into a Court which amounted to a small town *café* of ill-fame.

This must be borne in mind when we judge her, and we must also bear in mind the nature of the man who became her husband. Grand Duke Peter, aged sixteen, was the best instrument whom the fates could have chosen to add evil influence to that of the Russian

After Lambi

CATHERINE THE GREAT

Court, and to destroy such character and idealism as might reside within the breast of Catherine. Peter was practically mad, and he had been made mad by his education.

At the age of seven he was taken away from the care of women and handed over to officers of the Holstein guards, who taught him how to handle a gun and made him a sergeant. It was they, no doubt, who infected his mind with the passion for troops that filled his life, and which is described as "corporal's mania." He could never sit with his book if he heard the sound of military music; his greatest pleasure was a review; he collected uniforms. Meanwhile he was being educated in Swedish, in Russian, in Latin, but his principal tutor treated him so brutally that the child became unable to eat, and vomited at meals; this disability was treated by further punishment, and Peter was deprived of food. Punishments that we should not think of were inflicted upon him. Not only was he often whipped, but he was made publicly to kneel with a painting of a donkey round his neck, and sometimes he was made to kneel upon hard peas. No one ever used with Peter suasion or gentleness. He was weak; he was ill; early he learnt to drink, and as soon as he was released from his enthralment, learnt debauchery.

This was the poor creature to whom was to be handed over a princess who might have been brilliant. Catherine was not faithful to him, and that is not wonderful, for fate piled cruelly upon Peter; soon after his marriage he contracted small-pox, which was treated in the imbecile manner of that period, by bleeding and strong wine. He was hideous in mind, hideous in body, a creature hardly a man.

Yet for seventeen years Catherine lived with him. Loathe him and fear him as she might, she was bound to him by an imperial tie, one which she could not break, for neither Russia nor her Prussian parents would have received her back. She remained the creature's wife, and nine years after the wedding bore him a child. Here it is well to say that, though Catherine was unfaithful to her husband, the child was certainly his, even though by this time she had come into contact with a man of a certain charm called Saltykov.

While the Grand Duke was playing with dolls and arranging a marionet theatre, while he was boring holes in the door of the Empress Elizabeth's apartments to spy on her when she dined with her favourites, while he was behaving like a pervert and an idiot, Catherine, with her enquiring mind, with her taste for Western culture, was alone in a barbarous Court, and naturally she listened to Saltykov. She was not much over twenty, she had gaiety, and it may be that Saltykov loved her, not only because she bore a crown, but because she attracted him as a woman. Saltykov openly made love to her, gave her the illusion of the grace which she hoped to find in a man. For eight years he cheered her, and during that time she was faithful to him. Meanwhile, the Grand Duke was not troubling, for he did not care how his wife amused herself provided he might do so too. But it is only a little later, in regard to Poniatovsky, that we realise the full measure of the baseness of Peter.

Catherine was popular; Catherine was important. She was the mother of the heir to the Russian throne, and if he died it was to her that the throne must look, and the child was obviously Peter's—no son of Saltykov could have been so ugly or so devoid of wits. Therefore she had more freedom of movement; she did not have to hide her pleasures so carefully as in the days of Saltykov. Thus she was a centre of intrigue, because she had a great personality. It is said that the dominating minister of that day sought for her a lover, one of his creatures. But just then there arrived in St. Petersburg Count Stanislaus Poniatovski, who soon after became Minister Plenipotentiary of Poland. Here was an entirely new type of man; here was a man of whom she had dreamed, noble in demeanour, though rather sombre, endowed with ticklish pride, and very fastidious in the company he kept. He was a gentleman; he established a sharp contrast with the drunken and debauched Russians. His speech was gentle, and, though his education was not very good, his manners were excellent.

Quickly Catherine fell in love with this man, and, so far as can be told from their correspondence, we cannot quite say that he loved her, but we can say that he admired her. He writes a charming description of her, alludes to her good sense. It was the misfortune of Catherine to love rather than to be loved, but appreciated she could be. Poniatovski was perhaps the first man to appreciate her, while Saltykov had used her only as the decoration of his pride. It is Poniatovski, we have said, who gives us the full measure of Peter's vileness. If Catherine was unfaithful to Peter, he had certainly given her the example. Openly he maintained Elizabeth Vorontzoff as his mistress.

On a particular occasion, when Poniatovski unexpectedly called upon Catherine, Peter, who was well aware of the relationship and viewed it with indifference, insisted upon waking up Catherine, who was asleep, and arranging a supper-party for the four. It was a gay supper-party, at the end of which Peter withdrew with Elizabeth Vorontzoff, saying to his wife and her lover: "Well, children, I don't think you require our company any longer." If Catherine's love-life is adjudged against her, it cannot be said that either by example or precept was she assisted in any other.

The Empress Elizabeth died, Peter came to the throne, and with him Catherine. Peter did nothing to raise the prestige of Russia. His promotion he looked upon merely as a means of gratifying himself, while escaping censure, spending more money and drinking more wine, flaunting his mistresses more openly.

But Catherine had by now established her influence and gained a certain respect. Many members of the solid classes, and a proportion of the army, hated Peter. The army hated him mainly on account of his "corporal's mania," the constant parading and reviewing, and the brutality of his rule. Many who did not hate him despised him; even his friends despised him, and remained his friends only so as to use him. Among these Catherine found supporters, notably the five brothers Orloff. These were led by Gregory Orloff, who became Catherine's lover, and clung together in an alliance of exploitation which lasted nearly twenty years. They were not clever;

they were essentially boorish aristocrats, more boorish than the aristocrats described by Serge Aksakoff in *A Russian Gentleman*. But they loved power; they realised that Peter the imbecile must soon die, and that Catherine would be the natural regent of the realm while her child was in infancy.

Peter was the only impediment between them and supreme power, for Gregory held Catherine, and the brothers Orloff held Gregory. Thus, suddenly, came the *coup d'état*. Rebellious troops, headed by the Orloffs, surrounded Peter, who was forced to abdicate, craven, weeping, begging for his life, offering bribes, even appealing to God—he who had raised a party against him by blatant defiance of religious ordinances. And the miserable Peter did not survive, for he was murdered by Alexis Orloff, after which a bulletin was issued stating that he had died of apoplexy. The murder was an incident in which Catherine had no share. At the age of thirty-three she was Empress of Russia.

Catherine as Empress certainly set before herself the model of Peter the Great. She was, like Peter the Great, like Elizabeth, a woman who did not stand upon her dignity; she preferred the people to the nobles, and she honestly attempted to bring in modern culture and Western agricultural methods. An even more interesting move was the suppression of slavery in the mines. Catherine suppressed this traffic, and though this measure was immediately followed by riots and insurrections, fermented on one side by the mine-owners, who saw their labour lost, on the other by the miserable peasants themselves, who feared that this tragic labour would be replaced by torture, she triumphed by military means. She proved to Russia that someone had come to the throne who might think wrong, but who at least thought—who might will unwisely, but who could will.

Tyrannical, well-meaning, sensual, and courageous, Catherine was remarkable. And what was more remarkable was her inclination towards the intellectual ferment of the eighteenth century. She corresponded with Voltaire, with Grimm; she offered Diderot the post of librarian at the court. Herself without faith, she had an absurd vision of Russia suddenly waking to the cult of reason, and giving up what Russia called her religion—a jumble of Greek Orthodoxy, of eastern fairy-tales, and of bogies watching by the wayside. "The Semiramis of the North," as Grimm called her, had come too soon in the history of her country.

It is not wonderful, in these circumstances, that Catherine met problems. Difficulties enough might be amassed by her passion for modernity; greater difficulties were brought into being by her favourites. It was impossible for Catherine to marry again. If she sought a husband among powerful kings or heirs to thrones, such as those of Denmark, Sweden, Turkey or France, the unity of the Russian realm would never be achieved, and the most grave dynastic results would follow.

The Russians, being a Slavic and a barbarous people, would never have looked upon the foreign husband as being merely the consort of their Empress. Any husband of Catherine would have been looked upon as Tsar. Being a foreigner, he might have aroused great dislike. One of the palace revolts, which had made Catherine as they had made her predecessor, Elizabeth, would have resulted in her overthrow. Also, there were religious difficulties; no Greek Orthodox prince was available; the people would not have accepted a Roman Catholic from France or Poland; still less would it have been possible to arrange the ideal alliance—namely one with a Turkish prince.

All this has much to do with the psychology of Catherine, of which something must now be said. She led a long and immoral life, but not more immoral than that of the average crowned head in her period. Catherine was lonely. One feels pity for her, seated upon her barbaric throne, born much too early. She is surrounded by a Court the licentiousness of which has become traditional. Her courtiers generally smell of drink or of the stables; while her taste inclines her to the irony of Voltaire, she is confronted with people in whom humour takes the form of a booby-trap.

This woman has to live sixty-seven years in this atmosphere with nothing to cheer her save an idiot child. It is not wonderful that Catherine, placed as she was, sought consolation. If she could find a delicate and chivalrous nature like Poniatovski, so much the better. If she loved any man it was Poniatovski, and she proved this affection by placing him on the throne of Poland. But she could not hope everywhere to discover so fine a flower. Needing solace, needing love, like a natural, commonplace woman, needing the reinforcement against age which the love of a man affords, shut off from marriage, deprived of normal maternity, it is natural that Catherine, the proud Empress, should have flung herself at the knees of a coarse man like Orloff, begging him to love her, or at least to pretend, begging him to bring into her life, if not love, then its illusion, so that she might not always sit alone among the ice of the Neva, upon a throne as cold.

The books and plays which represent Catherine as a wanton have exaggerated a moderate amount of truth. All through her history Catherine distinguished herself from Elizabeth by choosing, if not men of attainments, at least men not without certain military capacity. Seeking among poor material, she took the best she could find.

Certainly her habit, which was to promote a discarded favourite to high position, to make him chamberlain, general, or governor suggested the attitude of a rich man who pensions off a woman who has ceased to please. It suggests the attitude of a sultan. But, in fact, it reveals sweetness in the character of Catherine. If she had invariably promoted to high places the men whom she favoured at the time, one would understand that here was merely the effect of an exuberance of love, but she did not always do that; indeed, it was generally after the attraction had waned, in an outburst of gratitude, in an outburst of kindly feeling, she gave a solid souvenir of wealth, and rank to the man who had once held the affections of his sovereign.

Of all these favourites Orloff was the most important, because he, longer than any, controlled her regard. He was a very big man, notorious for bravery in the field; his countenance, with its long, bent nose, its hard chin, and indented forehead, had an air of mercilessness. He was not exactly stupid, having the cunning of the savage, but he was illiterate to the last degree. He could read, he could write, these were his modest accomplishments, and it is pathetic to record that Catherine for a long time strove to educate him, to make him understand, not only the importance of spelling and the desirability of cultivating table manners, but also the philosophic ideas of the eighteenth century and some of her religious scepticism. She might as well have spared the effort: in vulgar parlance, "one cannot teach tricks to a silly monkey."

Orloff did not survive her; indeed, after some years, though he retained over her a certain influence, she allowed him to marry a certain Miss Zinovieff, who was only fourteen, and for whom he had conceived a passion. Orloff, after five years of matrimony, lost his young wife, as a result of which he became insane and died. It is one of the tragedies of Catherine that for her sake no man became insane and died.

Indeed, she was too set apart from common passions, being now unquestioned master of the throne. Some years after her accession Ivan III, the unfortunate heir, whom Empress Elizabeth had deposed, died after twenty years of solitary confinement. It cannot be said that Catherine connived at his assassination, but the malcontents of the kingdom saw in the miserable prisoner a symbol about whom they could rally to overthrow Catherine, and to instal themselves at Court. Headed by a half-crazy officer called Mirovitch, they attempted to rescue Ivan III. Since Catherine had given instructions that he must be slain rather than allowed to escape, in the course of the attack the assassination was performed. Catherine was not to blame, but this gave her Russia, which she held in peace and power for over thirty years.

Meanwhile, Catherine continued her wearisome career among lovers who did not love her ; as the power of Gregory Orloff waned others, such as Vassiltchikoff and Potemkin, enjoyed the favour of the Empress.

Potemkin is by far the most interesting of Catherine's lovers. He reached a height of cynicism which Gregory Orloff did not attain. He obtained the favour of Catherine simply enough, by vowing that he adored her and making public the fact that he suffered from a hopeless passion. Catherine could never resist this, for her vanity was immense, and Potemkin, though hardly dowered by nature, was a gallant soldier. He was an ugly man, with fat, pendulous cheeks and a very long nose, but there is a hint of humour in his face ; one may believe that he amused the Empress, and that his cynical attitude offered her a slight, attractive reflection of what she enjoyed in Voltaire. She promoted him, following on his successes in the Turkish wars, and for fifteen years he was not only her mental anchor, but her most powerful minister.

Potemkin was a real Russian, intensely extravagant, fond of pageantry, debauched, attracted by any pleasure and entirely irresponsible—one could not tell whether he would break his word, deny what he had spoken before a score of witnesses, or whether he would beggar himself in light generosity.

But where Potemkin is interesting, and where the tragedy of Catherine appears, is in his attitude to favourites. He realised that he could not indefinitely hold the Empress as a lover, so decided to provide her with young and attractive officers who would keep her amused, just as he would have given her dolls if she had been a child. He himself chose them; it was Potemkin brought to Catherine Zavadovsky, Zoritch, Korsakoff, Lanskoy, Yermoloff, Monomoff, and others. This man of inconceivably cynical mind removed any man in whom Catherine showed too much interest, because he feared that he might obtain power over her. If one pleased the Empress too well Potemkin degraded him if he was weak, promoted him if he was strong. Was he a soldier? He could be given a command, make war in the Crimea. Was he an official? An excellent post fell vacant not far from the Caucasus. And was he a nuisance, such as Lanskoy? Potemkin had him poisoned.

Yet these turbid years were not without their historical magnificence. Loose as she might be, and often foolish, Catherine had set before herself an imperial ideal rather akin to that of Cecil Rhodes. She wanted to Russianise the East, just as Cecil Rhodes desired to Anglicise Africa. The Russia of her period was not the vast empire which entered the war of 1914. Against its western frontiers it found Sweden, a powerful empire spreading into Finland; it found Courland and the Baltic provinces shutting off Russia from the sea; it found a distracted Poland torn with dissensions, but still a strong Roman Catholic buffer against the typical Russian Orthodox. Also there was Austria, the land which used to be called the Empire, and, above all, there was Turkey in the south.

The Turkey of the eighteenth century, heir of Soliman the Magnificent, was not the wretched remnant which now haunts south-eastern Europe. The

Turkey of that day comprised the whole of the Balkans—modern Turkey, Serbia, Greece, Albania, most of Bosnia, Bulgaria, Roumania, Bessarabia. Through its vassal, the Khan of Crimea, it controlled all the south of Russia up to the Ukraine, while Asia Minor, Syria, and Egypt provided a great reservoir of fanatical Moslem troops.

Catherine, master of her advisers, did nothing so foolish as to quarrel with Sweden. Peter the Great had settled the account of Charles XII of Sweden, at Poltava, in 1709. Fairly safe on her northern border, Catherine set herself two tasks; one was to develop her empire towards the west, to make it contiguous with Prussia, and thus to allow the easy entry of liberal ideas; the other was to crush the Turk, lest the Turk should crush Russia. It was during her reign that developed the urge of Russia towards Constantinople and the Ægean Sea, an urge which produced the Crimean War in 1854, the further war which was ended by the Congress of Vienna in 1878, and perhaps to an extent the war of 1914.

So the Turkish war comes, but results only in pushing back a little further the southern borders of Russia. In the days of Catherine Russia reaches the Dniester, but one important thing happens: as Russia marches south the oppressed peoples of the Balkans begin to conceive hope, they see the Christian power approaching, and are nerved to organisation. It is the march of Catherine into the south that will, two generations later, give the Greeks strength to rid themselves of the Turks.

In Poland the reaction was different, and for

sentimental reasons, which the writer cannot understand, Catherine has been represented as a plotter and a conspirator against an innocent little country. In this case her main object was to forbid the re-creation of a Poland which was the historical enemy of Russia, which once had been strong, and might be strong again.

In fact, wretched Poland was in dissolution, and Catherine gave it its last blow. The nobles were so strong that no king could assert himself; the royal house of Poland disappeared, and was replaced by elected kings, who in view of their election had no power. And the chaos was so great that at one time no law could be passed in the Polish Parliament if one nobleman objected to it. A system so imbecile, an obscurity so intense, would have resulted all by itself in the downfall of the Polish nation. Catherine understood this, and, since she could not acquire Poland for herself, became the head of the conspiracy with Austria and Prussia which annexed one, then another, and yet another portion of Poland, until that country became nothing more than a geographical expression.

Catherine grew old, Catherine was secure upon the throne, every year more glorious, and yet she was not entirely recognised as equal among kings. Hence, at the last minute, the king of Sweden refused to marry her granddaughter, and Catherine wept. She was growing old, she had achieved much, but she had never been loved. She had taken too much of the pleasure of life from the hands of men, not enough from the soul which should have been strong. At sixty-seven she still had a favourite, Planton Zuboff. She died as a foolish old woman, grimacing into the eyes of a young man, hoping that she still was fair, begging him to call her fair, and believing him when he lied.

A strange woman, a woman not without nobility. The present writer likes best to think of Catherine of Russia when she reproved Prince de Ligne. The young Frenchman, having discovered some Mussulman women unveiling because they thought themselves alone, hurried back to ask some of the courtiers to come with him and enjoy this piquant spectacle. Just as Queen Victoria, in rather a similar case, remarked, "We are not amused," Catherine showed a dignity of mind which perhaps sums up a woman of composite mind: "Gentlemen," she said, "this pleasantry is in very bad taste, and sets a very bad example. You are in the midst of a people conquered by my arms; and I propose that their laws, their religion, their morals, and their prejudices shall be respected."

Born a hundred years later, in a country more favoured by education, Catherine would have made a great constitutional queen. But perhaps she would not have enjoyed it.

BIBLIOGRAPHY

The Life of Catherine the Great of Russia, by E. A. Brayley Hodgetts.

The Comedy of Catherine the Great, by Francis Gribble.

Monograph on the Reign of Catherine the Great, by Waliszewski.

Memoirs of Catherine the Great.

MADAME DE MAINTENON

VIII. MADAME DE MAINTENON

VICTORY BY VIRTUE

Not all lovers are sinners, and in the present series it has been the care of the writer to illustrate, together with the glowing amours of Mary Stuart and the sordid intrigues of Lady Hamilton, the domestic graces of Queen Victoria, and now the virtue of Madame de Maintenon, which led her, if not to the throne, then to marriage with a king. Though Madame de Maintenon lived to the age of eighty-four, not a word can be said against her repute. Always faithful, always religious, always dutiful, she exceeded perhaps only in virtue. She was a curious product of the eighteenth century, when modesty and morality were somewhat detrimental in a lady of quality. She would have been a more normal occurrence about 1840, when she would have worn a good black silk frock, so thick that it could stand up all by itself, and good black Victorian principles, equally capable of maintaining an erect attitude.

It is this virtue, no doubt, which has done Madame de Maintenon some harm. There is a point at which fidelity, honesty, and chastity become repulsive; since people like Madame de Maintenon must go to their confessor and, week after week, year after year, declare themselves sinless, we feel that something has been left out of their composition. Hence we find Sir

James Stephen describing her as "intriguing, selfish, narrow-minded, and bigoted."

One understands that point of view. There was about Madame de Maintenon nothing fascinating; her eyes did not slay, though they were fine and black; her hair, that was also fine and black, was no mesh to trap sunshine and entangle sinners. She had beautiful hands, a fine stately figure, but she was not good-looking. A fine forehead, a heavy, rather shapeless mouth, and a thick nose—all this hardly prepared her to be the wife of Louis XIV, one of the most abandoned and debauched connoisseurs of feminine beauty who have sat upon the French throne. She must have had some secret charm, and the writer presumes that this charm arose from a fine, clear intelligence, from religious views, which were certainly narrow, but which were held calmly, and also from a certain personal courage which bade her confront peacefully gorgeous courtesans like the Montespan and the Fontanges. There was nothing rugged about her; she was like a placid and broad river which inexorably flows towards the sea.

But, before developing the story of Louis and Madame de Maintenon, we must indicate not only the origin of the heroine, but also the atmosphere in which she had her being, because this profoundly affected her character and her proceedings through life. She was born as Françoise d'Aubigné in 1635, and it is interesting to observe that she was born in prison, where her father, the Protestant Constant d'Aubigné, had been imprisoned by the King. "From prison to royalty" therefore serves as a motto for Madame de

Maintenon. The reader should, however, not conclude that her father was one of those heroic Protestants who dared to set up their small band against the Catholic King. Constant was entirely worthless, dissipated, flighty, and a Protestant only because his family were Protestants. Also, he inherited the curse of his father because he betrayed him to the French King, and, to obtain favour, dispossessed the old man of his lands.

His blood never influenced Françoise; she was a true descendant of her grandfather, Agrippa d'Aubigné, one of the most prominent leaders of the fighting Protestants, who, by speech, by writing, and by constancy in misfortune, had provided a rallying-point in the west of France. He is intensely puritanic, detesting the snares of this world, passionate for pure living, and none too friendly to the arts. That fierce Puritan stock which produced the pioneers of New England and the Presbyterians of John Knox, ran in Madame de Maintenon's veins—and met there in the most unexpected manner the Catholic blood of her mother, Jeanne de Cardhilhac. For Constant, while in prison, enlivened his captivity by fascinating and marrying the daughter of his gaoler. Passionate Puritan on one side, ardent Catholic on the other, here was indeed a mixture as explosive as the gipsy and Puritan strains which made Jane Welsh Carlyle.

So much for her heredity, but her surroundings were equally stimulating and tragic. For over a century France had been ravaged by the religious wars between Protestants and Catholics; the throne was then endangered by the civil war known as the Fronde.

Protestants had been besieged at La Rochelle by that flail of the Roman Church, Richelieu, and they had been massacred on St. Bartholomew's Day. At last a certain toleration had been brought in by the Edict of Nantes, and just then Protestants might go their way unmurdered, but vexed by the local authorities, the tax-gatherer, and society.

The question was not settled, and during Madame de Maintenon's lifetime it was to rise again when the Edict of Nantes was revoked, and the distracted Protestants fled to England, Holland, Switzerland—even as far as America and the Cape of Good Hope. Into this chaos had crept strife within the Catholic Church, strife between the Jansenists, who based their faith upon the moral life, and the Ultramontanes, who gave allegiance only to the Pope. The seventeenth century was a period of intense mental agitation, preparing the great movement of the eighteenth century that was to produce Voltaire, the French and the American Revolutions. It was a fine atmosphere for a woman of character, and Madame de Maintenon comported herself in such a way as to make her name historic.

The early part of her life was as painful and as uncomfortable as life can be. By her mother's wish she was baptised as a Catholic, but, having among her relatives an aunt called the Marquise de Villette, who had power and wealth, she was brought up by the Marquise as a Protestant. Her mother passionately resented this, and the child was constantly argued with, bribed, terrorised, by these warring relatives. No doubt this conflict of views tended to develop her, to force her to take her own religious line. She became nominally a Catholic, but actually there always ran through her mind much of the sobriety and the affection of clean-living which accorded with the Protestant outlook.

Finally, at fifteen, another aunt intervened, this one a Catholic, Madame de Neuillant, who placed her in a convent. It is a testimony to the importance which was then attached to every individual in this struggle between two versions of a single faith that a nun took the trouble to arrange a debate between a Catholic doctor and a Protestant pastor, merely to secure this child of fifteen. At the end of this debate Françoise declared herself converted a Catholic, and so she remained all through her life, reserving, however, much of the spirit of free self-examination which the Ultramontane Catholics so much feared.

Unfortunately, Madame de Neuillant, pre-occupied as she was by her niece's soul, took very little interest in her worldly welfare. The girl had no effective parents ; she was practically a poor relation, and Madame de Neuillant, having secured her for the Catholic faith, promptly decided to be rid of a growing girl who would no doubt become a nuisance. Françoise was offered the alternative of a convent or marriage, this being the usual choice set before a girl in that period. It is not known whether she hesitated much, but it is unlikely. Though she was deeply religious, her instincts took her towards the world ; she was active, not contemplative, and so she chose marriage.

No more terrible marriage could have been prepared than the union between young Françoise and old

Scarron. No one, save a woman who wished at any cost to be rid of a girl, would have consented to such a match as Madame de Neuillant organised. Scarron was not only old enough to be Françoise's father, but he was paralysed, a creature whom people moved about from his chair to his bed, who retained of manhood only a fairly nimble wit, a capacity for light verse, and, unfortunately, no great capacity for securing a small fortune to his widow. She lived with him for eight years, until he died, and it must have been a strange household, for the man was loose, fond only of gaiety, while his wife was grave, pre-occupied with moral theories. It is believed, however, that he appreciated her, that he respected her, for he applied to her the following lines :

> She whom heaven chose my anguish to allay,
> Deserves a better mate and eke a fate more tender.

She was a good wife to him ; she did not too often censure the licence of speech which reigned among his friends ; she accepted as a task set by heaven the care of this invalid, and though she tried to turn his mind to the world with which he must make his peace, she was not unkind. Indeed, she mourned him dutifully, though he left her in extreme poverty. But he had done her his first and last service in dying, releasing her into troubled France, no longer as a defenceless girl, but as a widow. By being married she had gained her status, and she was better fitted for the world as the cripple's widow than as a lonely maiden.

Fortunately, Scarron had made a reputation, and since Louis XIV favoured the arts he granted a pension to Madame Scarron. In that sense he was rewarded for much good that he had done to French literature by protecting Corneille, Molière, Racine, Boileau, and many others, for he gained the distant regard of the woman who was to soothe his last years.

Madame Scarron would gladly have lived peacefully upon her small pension, but the friends of Scarron, who respected and liked her, did not forsake her when her husband died. She retained the aristocratic contacts her husband had enjoyed, and eventually, through the influence of these surroundings, found herself at Court in the anomalous position of governess to the illegitimate children of the King.

Of Louis XIV much might be said, and he must not be judged as would be a monarch of the present day. Morally speaking, he was not much better, not much worse, than the average crowned head of his period. Married for purely political reasons, he saw no reason why he should refuse himself the liberty accorded to royalty. Throughout his long life—until, indeed, Madame de Maintenon establishes her influence—the emotional history of Louis is a story of favourites, who live at Court, who meet the Queen, whose wishes prevail while those of the wife are set aside. Their illegitimate children are born; indeed, seventeen are credited to the King. These women, particularly Madame de Montespan, become so powerful that they are respected and courted so much more than the Queen that the latter ceases to count; it is the courtesan who can confer promotion in the army or official rank.

Louis was not only a sensualist, but also a man of considerable attainments. If he had not been ridden by ambition he would not have left France in the state of poverty and disaster to which it was reduced by the constant wars with the Germans, Austrians, and English. It was his vanity interfered with his otherwise brilliant abilities. He had a medal struck where he was represented as Apollo driving the chariot of the sun; he accepted the surname of the Sun King. Once, when in an argument, a councillor pleaded the interests of the State, Louis replied: "The State, that is me." He was a protector of the arts, and to him we owe what may be the golden period of French letters, because he developed to a great extent the system of patronage which, throughout his century and the next, enabled literature and painting to live. From the religious point of view, he was rather akin to Henry VIII. He was anxious that the faith should be strong, but he desired that loyalty to the King should stand before loyalty to the Pope. He promoted the Gallic Church as a part of the Church of Rome—yes, but as a part of the French realm first.

Such a man was ill-designed by nature to feel the attraction of Madame de Maintenon, but he was well-designed to realise her mental qualities. Louis was not a fool, and until the end of his life, when he grew obstinate and rather childish, chose his Ministers well. Colbert and Louvois were notable men. Twrenne and Condé were brilliant generals. In soldiers, politicians, and in writers Louis was a connoisseur. No doubt this explains the domination of Madame de Maintenon. He appreciated her brain.

If Madame de Maintenon (a name which she adopted in 1675, when the King gave her the estate so called) had been a fool, she would have attempted to establish herself at Court by competing with Madame de Montespan. She was young enough to vie with the great courtesan; she might, through her contacts with the King, have aroused his interest, and if she had done this we should know her only as one of the many women attached to the reputation of Louis XIV. But that was not her object; she was no coquette; she did not desire elevation in rank as passionately as she wished to preserve her virtue. Hence, she devoted herself entirely to the education of the children, and especially to the leading of her own religious life.

Madame de Maintenon's position was slightly uncomfortable; though the favourite reigned at Court, Madame de Maintenon was constantly haunted by the feeling that the King was doing a great wrong to the Queen. She was enough of her century to tolerate the situation, but she adopted as a mission that she must reconcile the King with the Queen, and bring them to live together again in Christian matrimony. This had a great bearing upon her career, because the pious party at the Court saw in her a powerful ally. Not all the nobility condoned the behaviour of Louis XIV; many, particularly those who were attracted by the moral ideas of Jansenism, wished to make an end of this scandal. Finding in Madame de Maintenon a woman who thought as they did and had power ready to hand, they rallied about her, and owing to them she stayed at Court.

She did not like the position. She was not sure that it was correct, even if it was moral, to condone by her attention the existence of Madame de Montespan's children. She lived with them in semi-seclusion, and perhaps Madame de Montespan resented this, for they gave to Madame de Maintenon a love which their mother did not deserve, but which she wanted all the same. Also, they saw too much of each other. The Montespan wished to treat Madame de Maintenon as an inferior; she even tried to marry Madame de Maintenon to an old man, so that she might leave the Court. However, she never went so far as to demand her removal; in fact, the King made it clear that, though he had regard for Madame de Montespan, he also had a regard for his children.

Meanwhile influences were working towards Madame de Maintenon. She had for an ally Bossuet, the most famous church orator France has known. As the King approached middle age Bossuet strove to detach him from Madame de Montespan. He did not succeed, but the King weakened. Though Mlle. de Fontanges was to replace Madame de Montespan, as the latter had replaced Mlle. de la Valliere, the time was approaching when Louis would think of the future state, and when he would turn away from a life too easy. Moreover, the power of Madame de Maintenon was increasing; the longer she stayed at Court, and the longer it was made clear that she was a pure and honourable woman, the more her struggle for power increased. Finally, as she reached the age of forty-five, she gained the highest honour, and became lady-in-waiting in the household of the Dauphin (heir presumptive) after his wedding to a Bavarian princess.

A woman other than Madame de Maintenon would have contented herself with a rise so dazzling, since a

P. Mignard

MADAME DE MAINTENON

position akin to this would have been accepted—indeed, sought for—by any French duchess. But honours did not appeal to Madame de Maintenon; she regarded exalted positions merely as opportunities to lead an exalted life and to induce others to do likewise.

For many years she had been under the influence of her confessor, the Abbé Gobelin, who found in her much of the Calvinistic tendency inherited from her Puritan grandfather, which was then manifesting itself inside the Catholic faith under the name of Jansenism. Madame de Maintenon found a natural appeal in the stress which Jansenism laid upon acts as opposed to faith. She was naturally a Protestant. But Gobelin made her understand that Jansenism was actually only the reply of common sense to the excesses of the Jesuits and of Molinos. Because the latter had carried the theory of the service of God to the point of what they called diplomacy, Jansenism turned too far from the duty of a faithful Christian and too near to the merely ethical life. Thus Madame de Maintenon was not only influenced, but by degrees introduced into the scheme of those members of the Court who proposed to celebrate the purification of Louis XIV by his reconciliation with his wife.

It was then that her power asserted itself. Lady-in-waiting to the Dauphine, she had constant access to the Court. She was there when Madame de Montespan was sent away, there still when Mlle. de Fontanges was created a duchess and likewise sent away. She had constant contact with the King, and he must have found charm in her conversation, since every day he spent at least two hours in her company. She talked to him of life and how it should be led; she discussed religion, and was wise enough to leave politics to him. She knew that she must take him by flattery, and she passionately desired to influence his mind. Naturally, intrigue was busy against her; those who had hoped to replace Mlle. de Fontanges proclaimed that she was now the King's favourite. Though she was forty-five, she was not sheltered against charges which are obviously absurd.

Yet Madame de Maintenon did not triumph too openly; she retained the semi-friendship of Madame de Montespan, and meekly bore the ill-will of the Dauphine, who did not like her. Always she concentrated upon the King, being virtually ruler of the household of the heir to the crown. Then events hurried: under the pressure of Bossuet and Madame de Maintenon the King was reconciled with his wife. Madame de Maintenon's work was done—at least so it seemed—when suddenly her labours had to be resumed: the Queen died, and the King was alone.

Here was indeed a terrible situation. Louis had been faithless enough while married, and had with difficulty been brought by fear of the other world to live for a while as a husband should. Now his wife was dead, and since he had heirs he need not remarry. "What," Madame de Maintenon asked herself, "would be his conduct now?"

The question was answered dramatically: she would marry him, and she herself would save him. Whether the idea came first to Louis or to Madame de Maintenon has been discussed, but it is much more likely that the nomination came from the religious party at Court. The Abbé Gobelin, the Bishop of Chartres—all who looked upon the Church as something between a collaborator and a controller of the King—realised that since Louis was only forty-five he might make another political marriage with some nonentity, who would either lack influence over him—as a result of which the reign of the courtesans would continue—or whose influence would be political rather than religious. Madame de Maintenon, who year by year had increased her power at Court, was the obvious alternative.

Within a few months of the death of the Queen Louis secretly married Madame de Maintenon, whom the Bishop of Chartres described to the King as "the helper whom heaven has been pleased to give you in the midst of the crowd of self-seeking and deceitful men who pay you court." She was forty-eight, and he was forty-five. It could not be a love match on either side, but it could be a union founded on mutual esteem: on the side of the King it was safety from the snares of the world, and salvation by virtue; on the side of Madame de Maintenon it was conquest for the spiritual realm of the greatest man in France. The nobility of her character can be gauged by the fact that she never boasted of her situation, never tried to assert her power. In secret she tended the children of the King, in secret influenced him in the direction she desired, and in secret she was his wife.

Whether the couple was happy is a matter of inference rather than statement. Neither was designed by nature to harbour a grand passion, for the woman was too rigid and the man too light, but there is no doubt that the thirty years during which they lived together cemented between them a bond so intimate—composed as it was of a joint aspiration to spiritual beauty, and a joint mission on politics—that we may certainly call this affection love. We know of only one quarrel between Louis and his wife, and it was a quarrel not devoid of important motives.

They quarrelled because Madame de Maintenon had not married the King merely to be his secret wife. She had married him to exercise power when she thought that it should be exercised, and that was in two directions. The first was the union of the Protestant and the Catholic Churches. The second was the development of female education in France. As regards these objects Madame de Maintenon was in the unhappy position of being a renegade Protestant, which meant that the Catholics did not entirely trust her, while the Protestants detested her.

However, it is certain that she was not responsible for the revocation of the Edict of Nantes, and for the emigration of the Protestants. She had been married only two years when this happened, and it is likely that Louis, in a fit of irritation, or because he could not brook in his realm the existence of people who thought differently from him, cancelled the Edict. By so doing he not only lost for France many of her most skilful artisans, especially weavers, but he reopened the wound which had been closed by toleration of the Protestant faith. Madame de Maintenon was always averse from violence. She believed in argument in bringing back the Protestants to the original faith.

Sometimes this led her astray, and made her ridiculous, for she did nothing to arrest the action of the absurd Converts' Bank, destined to assist Protestants who found themselves in a state of poverty, after seeing the light and rejoining the Catholic Church. A woman of her intelligence should have realised the absurdity of these methods of spiritual bribery. Her views, however, moderate as they were, led to her only quarrel with the King.

This quarrel arose actually from her educational activities. In the days of Madame de Maintenon there was for girls no education other than that of the convent. The education of chivalry had disappeared in the early sixteenth century, and since that time the nuns held firmly to what was called "feminine education," namely the cultivation of good manners and religious conformity.

Madame de Maintenon was so essentially a Protestant that, though she supported the Catholic religion, she was intimately irritated by such an education. She wanted a new type of girl, a girl well grounded in the faith, no doubt with the best manners, but above all a girl who would be of her own period. She did not want to produce women who knew nothing of modern literature; she did not care to have them sheltered so completely from knowledge of the world. She wished them to realise that passion, ambition, cupidity work in the human mind. She did not wish to throw them, as they were thrown, entirely ignorant into the arms of the men of the world. She converted the King to these ideas easily enough, because he had himself a taste for the arts, and out of this came

St. Cyr, the first French college for women that had any liberal spirit at all.

In that sense she was great, and for several years St. Cyr developed, gaining more and more pupils from noble families. The education went so far that the girls acted plays, a thing impossible in a convent. And it is not against Madame de Maintenon that in due course she became terrified by her own work. Finding that her pupils took too readily to passionate scenes, she tried to stop the movement she had initiated, and this gave rise to Racine's play, *Esther*, a sacred play suitable for girls intended to think correctly in spiritual matters. It is not against her, because we must not expect too much of pioneers. Indeed, if Madame de Maintenon had striven to create a school like the English Roedean, or a college like the American Ann Arbor, she would not only have proved ineffective, but she would have been monstrous.

It was the development of St. Cyr which produced domestic disunion. Since religion was, in that institution, not handed out in solid tabloids to be swallowed every day, the spirit of personal examination —which was moving all through the seventeenth century, which had created Pascal and Port Royal with its abstraction from the world, which had given birth to Jansenism and its stress upon works—could not leave aside such a college. The theological microbe which invaded it was called Quietism. This was a view held mainly by Molinos, according to which the final state of union with God is reached when the soul is in a state of perfect inaction ; in this union the soul is purely passive under the action of the divine light.

In other words, this was merely an evolution of the old contemplative theory which originated by stages from Plato.

If the introduction of Quietism had been effected with less *éclat*, all might have been well, but it was proclaimed by Madame de Maisonfort and her cousin, Madame de Guyon, proclaimed as such things are by women, intensely, intolerantly, and noisily. The air of Quietism was far from quiet; it was a screaming silence. Also, it gained the support of Fénelon, the greatest French prelate of the seventeenth century after Bossuet. Perhaps it was Fénelon caused the trouble, because the King might have ignored the ladies of St. Cyr, but the great archbishop was personally disagreeable to him, not because of his Quietism, but because he was an Ultramontane, because he looked to the Pope first and to the King second. Therefore, just as Molinos's *Spiritual Guide* had been condemned in 1687, the *Maximes des Saints* of Fénelon was also condemned, after he had been compelled to retract what he had there written. He was exiled to Cambrai in 1697, while Madame de Maintenon was blamed by the King for having caused dissension at St. Cyr.

She won him back, however, because she was always there, always calm, always dutiful, because he was growing old, and because he needed the constant reassurance of the soul. Also, it is likely that he was impressed by her ecclesiastical influence and by a small fact which shows him very human. A new Pope, Clement XI, was elected with the support of the French party; in 1700 he wrote to Madame de Maintenon a letter thanking her for her services to the faith. Since the Pope had been a Louis candidate he must think as Louis thought: therefore, if the Pope approved of Madame de Maintenon, then the King approved. Louis set up a Pope as his creature, and then believed in him.

So, in the twilight of their years, those two, the most notorious King in French history and the woman who had crept into Court as the governess of his illegitimate children, grew old in peace and in mutual confidence. They were terrible years, for Louis in his dotage grew more and more subject to flattery, so that the generals whom he chose were more and more incompetent. The French arms, which had been victoriously led into Germany, were now on every quarter menaced by German, Austrian, British arms. The finances were in chaos. Pestilence and famine joined with hard winters to prepare the discontent which was to break out within three generations.

And not only was the realm rocking, but, one after the other, the sons of Louis died, all of small-pox. Within one year three were made Dauphin, and three died. We can neglect the rumour according to which they were poisoned by the Duc d'Orléans, nephew of the King and the future regent; it may have been so, but that does not concern us. It is enough that more and more the King spent his time with his wife, who alone could distract his thoughts and beguile the tedium of the last years of a sensual life. He died in 1715; his sons and their children, who had been under the influence of Madame de Maintenon, were dead; there remained some illegitimate children, too weak to help her, and there remained the Duc d'Orléans, who had always hated her, because she supported the King and his children, because she stood between him and the throne. He was regent for the infant King, Louis was dead, leaving her widowed at the age of eighty.

Without quarrelling, without struggling for a power which had gone, she retired to St. Cyr, where she spent her last years in dignity and in spiritual exercises. She asked nothing, she strove for nothing, she patiently awaited the call of God whom she had striven to serve, and whose mercy she approached with perhaps a little too much confidence. No doubt she felt that she could hold up her head before the judgment seat, declaring that in her long life she had made a school and saved a king.

BIBLIOGRAPHY

Louis XIV and Madame de Maintenon, by Blennerhassett.

Madame de Maintenon, by Taillandier.

Memoirs of Madame de Maintenon, by La Beaumelle.

Le Siècle de Louis XIV, by Voltaire.

NELSON AND LADY HAMILTON

IX. NELSON AND LADY HAMILTON

THE WILL TO POWER

Paris would have been a small creature but for Helen of Troy; Bothwell would be unknown but for Mary, Queen of Scots; if Nelson had not loved her we should not know the name of Lady Hamilton, that beautiful and light adventuress whose account on the rolls of history shows not one trait of decency. Because she was beloved of a hero she lives upon his memory like the parasite mistletoe upon the oak. Lady Hamilton sums up in herself the impertinence of beauty; re-arrange slightly the lines of her features, thin her hair, dull the glow of her eye, and history is changed.

Nelson goes down in history as one of its greatest naval commanders, but not as a romantic hero. The writer suspects that Lady Hamilton has done some good to the memory of Nelson; all men remember his famous signal: "England expects that every man will do his duty." We remember too a picturesque detail; Nelson, confronted by the craven signal of his superior officer, bidding him retire, placed the telescope which enabled him to read the signal to his blind eye. Picturesque, yes; but a matter of battles, not a matter of humanity. If Nelson had not associated himself with an infamous romance, he would not seem to us so human, therefore so real.

Indeed Emma Hamilton was such to change the

course of careers. We have many pictures of her, and in all she is radiant. The famous Reynolds, which depicts her as a bacchante, shows a broad face with a pointed chin, a nose slightly too long, but amusing, piquant, an adorable childishness in the moulding of the cheeks and eyes. . . . Petrarch wrote a sonnet to Laura's eyebrow: one wonders whether Laura's eyes equalled those of Emma—long eyes with enormous dark pupils, slightly deep-set, thus enabling the perfect long eyebrows to cast a beneficent shadow over these "mirrors of the soul," which in the case of Lady Hamilton mirrored nothing but vulgarity, common lust, and self-seeking.

She is more attractive still in Romney's picture, where upon her auburn hair lies a white hood. Here too are the immense eyes and the mouth where hides the damnation of men, a tender drooping underlip and a thick, avid, deliciously curved upper-lip. Under the hood she looks like a rebel saint, like one of those memories of female Christian missionaries which came in his sleep to tempt Saint Anthony.

These fine features, this air of aristocratic debauchery assists the legend of her birth. She saw the light, it is believed, in 1763 at Hawarden in Cheshire, in the home of Henry Lyon, a blacksmith, wedded to a village girl. In the late eighteenth century the condition of the English people was one of extreme coarseness, where in the midst of dirt and brutality meals were eaten off a wooden platter under the light of a candle made of animal fat. The promiscuity was intense, the moral level equal to that of the beasts. There would be no privacy, no facilities for cleanliness, no

George Romney

LADY HAMILTON AS DAPHNE

reading or writing, perhaps no religion—nothing but feeding, sleeping, and breeding. Though it is certainly not true that aristocratic circles produce a more refined type of beauty, it is certain that the conditions under which the gentle are bred go towards making their type more delicate, less essentially animal. Therefore there may be some truth in the legend that Mrs. Lyon was unfaithful to her husband the blacksmith, and that Emma was actually the offspring of Henry Cadogan, a scion of one of England's most distinguished families.

However, she stands in the parish register as the child of Henry Lyon, and as such she is brought up in poverty, in ignorance, and in dirt. Late in life she learns to write, and to the end of her life she cannot spell. For her there is no destiny—at least so it would appear—except to enter domestic service, to marry some coarse man, or perhaps, doomed by her beauty, to join the sorry sisterhood of the London streets. But beauty—that fatal enemy of the daughters of the poor—defeats itself when it strikes too hard at a victim. Had Emma Lyon been merely pretty, she could not have escaped, but beauty was piled so heavily upon that broad, low brow that she must emerge—emerge like a seed which forces its way through earth and through manure, benefiting by both.

For a while she followed her destiny. She became a servant, and no doubt she was petulant and untidy, because within her worked not only discontent with her conditions, but the immense consciousness which she carried to the end of her life: she was ambitious. Without realising it perhaps, she aspired to the protection of men, thus taking the only route open in those days to a woman. One gains an idea of her behaviour as a domestic through her dismissal from the house of Dr. Budd. There she found another maid, called Jane Powell, who shared with her a passion for acting, which actually expressed their desire to escape their lowly life.

Some short time after her engagement, when her master and mistress were out of the house, Jane dressed herself in Mrs. Budd's white satin wedding-dress, rouged her cheeks, and powdered her hair with flour. Meanwhile Emma draped her radiant tresses with a mantilla, removed all her clothing save a thin chemise, and, thus attired, danced as a nymph luring a satyr. They sang. They intoxicated themselves with movement. They were no longer servant-girls, but princesses. Then they were discovered. Dr. and Mrs. Budd discovered their establishment thus attired, thus performing, and the girls were dismissed.

Here was disaster, and Emma was not yet sixteen, still pure, still childish. No doubt it was her childishness led her into these first follies. Still she did not sink, for Jane Powell took her to see Sheridan, hoping to interest him in their desire to act upon the stage. Sheridan promised to give Jane a trial, but to Emma he offered only employment. Thus we find her in attendance upon Samuel Linley, who would gladly marry her, but Linley dies, and his parents drive her away, so that once more her only asylum is the street. So young, so lovely, and so poor, it is not remarkable that very swiftly Emma Lyon falls from the natural level of a young girl. A Mr. Angelo places her in the house of a certain Mrs. Kelly, a house of poor reputation, where dissipation and licentiousness make for the still innocent Emma a background which she cannot resist. She is admired ; she is hungry for life ; she realises that only through men can she triumph over circumstances.

It was thus that she met her undoing, for just then one of the friends of her childhood, Will Masters, whom she had known at Hawarden, fell into the hands of the press-gang. He was captured, as were so many Englishmen, and even Americans, in those days, by a posse of sailors, and recruited by force for the Royal Navy. Since the conditions of the Navy were then very hard, the press-gang was feared, and a pitiful message came to Emma. Among the friends of Mrs. Kelly was a certain Captain Payne, and to him, upon this errand of mercy, Emma went to seek the release of her old friend. But Payne was inflamed by her beauty, and, having her in his power, finding that within her warred the desire to save Masters and the desire to escape from her low conditions, he forced upon her attentions which she would have rejected had she been of single mind. Thus Payne became her first lover, and here was the end of one period, another beginning as she reached the aged of sixteen.

A curious side of Emma's character here appears : she could capture men, but she could not always hold them. Payne, who became the father of her first child—a child of which she rid herself by sending it to her parents at Hawarden—tired of her after a short time. And now Emma, having fallen from the state of labour, having acquired the habit of leisure, could not go back to the place whence she came. A man had taken her from domestic service, and other men must support her where he had placed her. Thus she is no longer virtuous, virtue having done for her much less than vice. For a while she assists in the ceremonies of a well-known quack, Dr. Graham. She appears in his reception-room, clad in flimsy draperies, representing the goddess Hygeia. There she encounters Sir Henry Featherstonehaugh, a fox-hunting squire and a boor by temperament, who takes her to his country seat, treating her half as a favourite, half as a domestic.

He does not matter, this man in whose heart echo only the barking of hounds and the chinking of tankards. He introduces Emma to the rougher side of the gentlemanly life. He has no conversation, save about beasts and bets. She is not revolted, for she knows no better, and yet there lives in Emma the aspiration which will now develop a tendency towards refinement and an appreciation of good manners. Without intellect, without good taste, without artistic feeling, she yet has an aspiration to good breeding. She likes men who do not swear in the presence of their womenkind, and who have not to be carried to bed after drinking two or three bottles of port. Having before she is twenty been the football in the game of fate, she is ready to develop on broader lines, and she meets Greville.

Charles Greville, a younger son of the Earl of Warwick, a man of fashion, fastidious in his clothing and in his speech, an educated man, who appreciates poetry and music, appears as a puzzling figure in the history of the woman who was to become Lady Hamilton. Greville appears to have been entirely without heart. He must have looked upon the radiant Emma much as he would have considered a picture. He would buy the picture for æsthetic reasons, and he would acquire the companionship of Emma for reasons hardly more ambitious. All through his life with her, which lasts until the beginning of her relationship with Sir William Hamilton, Greville treats her in a disdainful, casual manner. He makes her realise that to him she is a poor child born in the gutter, whom he has chosen to raise because he is a gentleman of taste, and because she pleases his eyes.

Not one letter of Greville's shows that he cared for Emma, that she was more to him than a fine piece of furniture. And we shall see a little further on to what cold depths of baseness Greville could descend. Indeed though there is little to be said in favour of Lady Hamilton, one might almost excuse her by contrasting her with Greville. So much younger than he, so poorly armed by education, so driven by her natural aspiration to comfort and to happiness, her mind offered itself as the natural victim of this cold and calculating man.

Very soon the relationship that established itself between Greville and Emma impressed itself upon Sir Henry. Following upon a violent quarrel, Emma was expelled from his regard. She flees to Hawarden, where she encounters with horror the poverty from which she sprang. She appeals to Sir Henry, who does not answer. At last she appeals to Greville, and she writes him a letter, ill-spelt and chaotic, which is tragic because it is genuine.

"Yesterday did I receive your kind letter. It put me in some spirits for, believe me, I am almost distracktid. I have never hard from Sir H., I have wrote 7 letters, and no anser. What shall I dow? O how your letter affected me when you wished me happiness. O, G. that I was in your posesion what a happy girl would I have been. Girl indeed! What else am I but a girl in distress—in reall distress? For God's sake G. write the minet you get this, and only tell me what I am to dow. I am allmos mad. O for God's sake tell me what is to become of me. O dear Grevell, write to me. Write to me. G. adue, and believe me yours for ever.

"Emily Hart.

"Don't tell my mother what distress I am in, and dow afford me some comfort."

Greville responded to this desperate communication. Having ruined Emma's position, he suggested that she should try to make up her quarrel with Sir Henry. He had had his sport, and did not wish to be worried with a woman who had amused him for a while, who after a while would weary him. However, she must have established some hold upon the emotions of Greville (for we may assume that the fishes have their passions), for soon after, perhaps because he feared scandal, he established Emma with her mother at Edgware Row, where she stayed for close on five years, partly under his protection and partly as his pupil.

For Greville had the taste of a gentleman, and, though gentlemen often fall under the sway of coarse beauty, they do not remain under it.

Greville admired Emma, admired her so much that he caused her to be painted, but he wanted her to be an intellectual companion fit for himself. Thus he caused her to take lessons in music and in dancing; he gave her lessons in English, and tried to teach her to spell. More effective still was the occasional companionship of the wits of Ranelagh. Being intelligent within a limited sphere, she gained from conversation and example much more than from books.

And she loved Greville so far as she could love. Strictly speaking, Lady Hamilton never knew the emotions of love, but she did, like a cat or a dog, feel some special kind of link with the person who afforded benefits. Just as a dog will whine and shows signs of delight when its master approaches with a plate of food, so did Emma give Greville such worship as was in her nature; she thanked him for money, fine clothes, pleasure, and idleness. Perhaps she felt for him more than for Nelson; she felt as much as she could.

However, her life with Greville was destined soon to end, not because she dissatisfied him, not because she wearied him, but because her protector was pursued by necessity. And, curiously enough, the necessities of Greville led to her fortune, indirectly to her historic renown. Greville, being a younger son, could expect only a pittance from his father, the Earl of Warwick. Therefore he had to make a career, and at the same time to secure from other branches of his family the fortune which he could not expect from his father.

The career he sought to make in politics, for which he was well-suited by a most acute and unscrupulous mind, he wished to reinforce by a rich marriage. Emma stood to a certain extent in the way of these ambitions. Though the eighteenth century was careless as to the morals of its politicians, though Prime Ministers took loose women publicly to the theatre, it would have been impossible for Greville to marry a girl of position and of fortune while maintaining Emma in Edgware Row. Once married, he could have created this establishment, but before marriage he had to be clear of entanglements.

All this worked upon him, upon his cold nature, and made him wish to be rid of Emma. Another thought operated, which was the desire to inherit from a relative the money which his father could not give him, and that relative was Sir William Hamilton, his uncle, who had a great affection for his nephew and proposed to make him his heir. When Sir William came to Edgware Row and was fascinated by Emma, it occurred to Greville that this worked towards his plans. He wished to get rid of Emma, and here was Sir William Hamilton much attracted by her. Why not give his uncle his desire, thus securing his good will, and at the same time entangle him with Emma, so that he could not marry again? Thus he would be quit of Emma, please Sir William, and prevent a new alliance which would deprive him of his chances.

This was a plan worthy of Machiavelli, and Greville found it easy enough to execute, because Sir William was at once bemused by the charms of Emma. He was elderly, over fifty, while Emma was hardly over twenty. He had a great position, being British ambassador to the kingdom of Naples and the two Sicilies; he was rich, a man of good breeding, a man who might rise higher in the king's service, a man of refinement and of good taste. Yet, like so many men of his type, he fell passionately in love with the entirely vulgar and self-seeking Emma.

However, Greville knew his uncle well enough to hide from him the ugly side of his scheme. Hamilton would never have lent himself to taking over his nephew's discarded mistress. In the card-rooms of London in those days it was common for a man to relieve another of an inconvenient woman in exchange for an excused gambling debt, and women were often bought and sold in this way for anything between five shillings and a thousand guineas. Hamilton would not have done that, partly because he was a gentleman and partly because he had attained the romantic age. In the fifties he could not do the crude things which appeal to the twenties; romance seldom begins to flower in a man before his fortieth year, and to Sir William, who had known only a rather official wife, the radiant young Emma represented romance.

So Greville, always subtle, took the opportunity to quarrel with Emma, accusing her of infidelity with Romney. Sir William's heart was touched by the nobility with which Emma repelled these charges. He wished to help her, to raise her, to rehabilitate her, and thus to see himself in the rôle of Perseus, rescuing Andromeda chained to her rock and waiting for the dragon. Besides, he was in love, and any excuse would serve to gain Emma's society.

When the situation was ripe, when Sir William realised that he could not do without Emma's company, Greville declared that Emma's education, Emma's progress in refinement could be secured only if she went with Sir William to the embassy at Naples. She was to go as a blend of companion, secretary, and ward, as a sort of dubious daughter. At least, that was her conception. On Sir William's side there was no intention to treat Emma except with the greatest respect. He loved her as a woman, but he wanted to love her as a daughter so long as she belonged to his nephew. There is much in Hamilton that we cannot understand and that seems contemptible, but essentially he was an exalted character, quixotic and absurd.

Curiously enough, Emma parted sadly from Greville, and he had much trouble to persuade her. Perhaps she loved him because he ill-treated her; perhaps, as suggested before, she was merely grateful. Perhaps, too, she was so much woman that she knew which way the journey tended, and turned to the young man rather than to the old. There were tears, protests, proclamations of passion; all this Greville received mercilessly, charging infidelity with Romney, sneering while Emma stormed. At last she agreed to go for six months, providing that Greville would then recall her. He never intended to do so. He intended to place half a continent between Emma and his career. He seldom answered her letters, or replied coldly as a pedagogue. She is pathetic then, when she writes to Greville:

"I have been from you going of six months, and you have wrote one letter to me, enstead of which

I have sent fourteen to you. So pray, let me beg of you, my much loved Greville, only one line from your dear, dear hands."

One would almost believe her to be genuine, and perhaps she was genuine while she wrote: there are such people. She was mourning Greville as she had mourned Featherstonehaugh, as later she mourned Nelson, as perhaps she mourned Hamilton. She was sincere—while her sincerity lasted.

But as the six months passed, as Greville remained cold, as she realised that all was finished, that now she depended entirely upon Sir William, and that the course which she had taken compelled her to depend upon some man, as the feelings of her protector grew unmanageable, as he came to love her so that he could not forgo her, she weakened. She did not gainsay Hamilton, and in 1785 it became known all through Naples that Sir William's lovely protégée now enjoyed all a woman can of a man's protection. Five years passed at Naples. Sir William, as he grew older, grew fonder, more intoxicated by this lovely childish creature, whose morals corresponded with her spelling. He knew her past, knew that before Greville Emma had accumulated experience of men, but it was so intolerable to him that he might lose her that he determined to make her entirely his. Greville defeated himself. He had wished to enthral his uncle, and he enthralled him so much that on the first of September, 1790, Sir William carried Emma back to London and made her his wife.

It should be said that when Emma, at the age of

twenty-seven, became Lady Hamilton she was a very different person from the uncouth wench whom Greville had begun to refine. Ten years of frequentation among men of culture, and even women of culture, since women were not particular in that century—and since it served many to remain on good terms with the British ambassador—had changed Emma. Though she could not spell, she had learnt a great deal—learnt not to boast; learnt never to ask an impertinent question; learnt to be silent; learnt above all to make friends with women as well as with men. She was socially veneered, and, though a certain coarseness always appeared, her loveliness and her rank excused her. She became an intimate friend of the Queen of Naples, and by so doing became the most powerful person in the kingdom.

The situation in the little kingdom was peculiar, and the next ten years, during which Lady Hamilton enjoyed the friendship of the Queen, were epoch-making years in history. They included the French Revolution, the coalition of the European kings to crush this revolution, so as to prevent in Europe the creation of a republic which they had been unable to prevent in America. As the revolution proved victorious, as the ragged, starving, ill-armed troops of France, intoxicated by the ideal of liberty, routed the royal troops, France became once more a power that counted in Europe. The revolution passed through the Terror, through an orgy of massacre, until at last the French people grew sick of slaughter, handed themselves over to a directorate of five, with whom was associated a great figure, Napoleon Bonaparte. Within the political sphere of Lady Hamilton this man became captain, general, consul. Between him and Nelson the struggle was set, because Napoleon radiated into Italy.

It is worth mentioning that Bonaparte affected Italy because he avoided the mistake made nearly twenty centuries before by the Roman emperors. While Rome played with Spain, Gaul, Asia Minor, Africa, and Egypt, she neglected the barbarians of Germany, Hungary, and Russia. Rome strove to make a strong empire, and left enemies upon her flank. Napoleon realised that revolutionary France, of which he was the heir, could not remain a self-contained entity, and that ultimately, if he failed to strike terror into the rest of Europe, Europe would overwhelm him. It was this which ultimately took Napoleon into Belgium and Holland—where upon the ice his cavalry captured a fleet—into Switzerland, Austria, Germany, and even Russia. It was this led him to Egypt, because thus he might sever the connection between England and India. It was this took him to Italy to establish first a Cis-Alpine republic of the north, later kingdoms north and south.

It was Napoleon therefore who forced upon the kingdom of Naples the necessity of an alliance with England. Because England was the country which Napoleon could not overwhelm, she became the mental asylum of the royal houses. In those days a country had to be with England or against her, and, though by degrees Napoleon forced his power upon Spain, and Naples too, compelling them to remain neutral, or to limit their assistance to the English, the yoke was uneasy. Queen Caroline of Naples was married to a rather foolish, vain man, King Ferdinand, who was only too glad to have the responsibility of power taken from him by an able wife. Since this wife became the intimate friend of Lady Hamilton, it is not wonderful that Lady Hamilton was able to affect the politics of the world.

Thus, in 1798, when Lady Hamilton was thirty-five, a little stouter than she should be, but as beautiful in her maturity as she had been in her girlhood, Napoleon prepared that attack upon Egypt which should divide the British from their possessions in the east. Once instal an army there, once expel all traces of British influence, and he would have reduced the British to communicating with India only round the Cape of Good Hope, an impossible undertaking. The expedition was prepared secretly, so secretly, covered by such clever misreporting, that he was able to assemble at Toulon the French fleet that should conquer Egypt. England heard of this too late, and Nelson, sent in pursuit, arrived at Toulon too late. The French had escaped him. He turned his ships to the south, but nowhere was there a port that could provide him with food and water, except Naples. France was inimical, Spain neutral, Northern Italy under French influence.

So to Naples he went, to be confronted with this difficulty: the kingdom of Naples had with France a treaty undertaking to supply never more than four British men-of-war, and here was a vast fleet—here the opportunity of England to win or lose a war. The action of Sir William Hamilton was not clear;

C. Lucy

NELSON ON THE EVE OF THE BATTLE OF TRAFALGAR

he had the diplomat's respect for treaties, and he was not instructed as fully as he might desire on British intentions as to Naples. If he procured the revictualling of Nelson he involved England with Naples more than might be desired. But Lady Hamilton had no such scruples. Partly out of patriotism, partly to assert her power, she went to Queen Caroline, and she found in her an enemy of the French. She stormed, she prayed, she wheedled a woman who was with her in her heart. What was a treaty to two women, one fanatical and one ambitious?

The British fleet was provided with all it needed, and Nelson sailed south, to the Battle of the Nile, one of the greatest battles of history, where he defeated the French by disregarding time and by attacking without deploying in the regulation manner. After the victory came the return of Nelson to Naples with his victorious fleet, to be nursed back to health by Lady Hamilton, to whom he owed his victory.

The royal house of Naples soon after paid for its falsity to its pledged word. The French were powerless at sea, but powerful on land, and soon Ferdinand and Caroline had to flee to Palermo under the protection of the British Fleet. Nelson, Sir William and Lady Hamilton went with them, and thus began the association which was to animate Nelson until his death.

It is well here to give a share to the character of Nelson. He was entranced by Lady Hamilton as other men had been, but it would be a mistake to regard him as a commonplace victim of a siren. Nelson was over forty, and, though he was married, had had many adventures. A popular sailor, a man of charm and of energy, he had found favour in the eyes of women. Thus he was a match for Emma, but he was no match for her charm. Until then he had dallied, and now he loved. Such glamour as attaches to Lady Hamilton is not her own; it is the passion of Nelson for her which illumines her memory, a passion which would have been fatal to a smaller man.

We may abandon the political side of the relationship by recording that after the insurrection of Naples and the coming of the French, Sir William Hamilton resigned his position as ambassador, and that King Ferdinand refused to support him, because he charged Hamilton with having broken his word to him in regard to the restoration of Malta. It is likely that the British Government was also anxious that Hamilton should forgo his position, owing to the open scandal of the relationship of his wife with Nelson.

The three had now become intimate friends. All three had gone to Palermo, and later Nelson accompanied the couple on their journey home. When, in 1800, they reached Yarmouth, it was to Lady Hamilton as much as to Nelson that went the plaudits of the crowd. It was known that she had assisted in the victory of the Nile, and, besides, the glory of the hero shed over her a golden dust. As for Hamilton, he was despised, as a man must be when he alone knows not of his wife's infidelity, and must still more be when it is believed that he knows.

Here we may say that the position of Sir William has never been made quite clear. It is much too lightly charged that he knew of the relationship between his wife and Nelson, and that he condoned it.

It is much more likely that a man of his character, who had taken Emma to Naples as a respectable ward, would believe that between Nelson and Emma existed only just such a friendship as he himself would have been capable of. Also he was over sixty, Emma was tempestuous, immersed in political intrigue, always in movement, fond of dancing and of entertainments. Perhaps she worried him, though he still loved her, and perhaps he was glad that Nelson should serve as a new interest, occupy her, and free him from the responsibility of entertaining her. And it may also be that in his eyes Nelson carried the attributes of divinity. Nelson's figure was so significant that Sir William may have accepted him as capable of no wrong.

Thus the astonishing story develops. Lady Hamilton returned to London, believing that she would be received with a cordiality akin to that of Naples. She did not realise that English morals were outwardly more severe than those of Italy. The Queen refused to receive her, not perhaps because she resented Lady Hamilton's past and Sir William's complacency, but because she considered that they had brought shame upon an English embassy. On the other hand, Lady Hamilton was admired by the Prince of Wales, an admiration encouraged by Greville, who naturally saw in this some means of advancing himself, and by Hamilton, who was under his nephew's influence. He would perhaps have been glad of new employment. But what is interesting in the acquaintance of the Prince of Wales and Lady Hamilton is the attitude of Nelson. He suffered when she came back to London, because he was afraid, faint and fond lover that he was, that in her own country the admiration which surrounded her would betray her and betray him.

The Prince of Wales terrified him because he knew Lady Hamilton's vanity and her ambitions. He trusts her and yet he does not. Thus he writes to her:

> "You are too beautiful not to have enemies, and even one visit will stamp you. He is without one spark of honour in these matters, and would leave you to bewail your folly. But I know you too well not to be convinced that you cannot be seduced by any Prince in Europe."

Later he wrote again:

> "I am so agitated that I can write nothing. I knew it would be so and you can't help it. Do not sit long at table. Good God! he will be next you, and telling you soft things. If he does, tell it out at table, and turn him out of the house. Oh God! that I was dead! But I do not, my dearest Emma, blame you, nor do I fear your constancy. I am gone almost mad, but you cannot help it. If I was in town nothing should make me dine with you that damned day. I have read your resolution never to go where the fellow is, but you must have him at home. Oh God! but you cannot, I suppose, help it, you cannot turn him out of your own house. If you cannot get rid of this, I hope you will tell Sir William never to bring the fellow again."

And yet he should have been sure of Lady Hamilton, for soon after was born their child, Horatia, whose

George Romney

LADY HAMILTON AS "THE SPINSTRESS"

parenthood was attributed to a certain Mrs. Thomson. The birth was kept secret, and Horatia was brought up under that assumed name. Naturally, the birth of his child had upon Nelson the effect of drawing him still closer to his beloved. Still at sea, he wrote to Lady Hamilton saying that he wished to resign his command, to take Emma and their child to Bronte, the Sicilian estate which King Ferdinand had given him. But here Emma showed that wisdom which always she had shown, attaching herself to the powerful and maintaining their power. She pleaded that Sir William was old, that he needed her; she had the hardihood to effect a dutiful spirit, directed towards her husband, in this a letter to her lover. What she wanted was to retain the shelter of Sir William's name and position, at the same time retaining the lustre shed over her by her relationship with Nelson. And Greville, still Greville, strove to prevent a decision so desperate, for this would bring to light the birth of Horatia, who, since the child was born in wedlock, would be his uncle's heir.

So Nelson remained in command because Emma bade him, and in the intervals of cruises returned to her. It was scandal, for he had bought at Merton a house where for some time he lived with both the Hamiltons. A man of smaller position would have been blasted by the ill-repute which spread about such an arrangement, but Nelson was beyond attack. Indeed, when Lady Hamilton became a widow in 1803, Nelson was striving for a divorce from his wife. He wanted to marry Emma, and this glowing destiny was denied her only by the death of Nelson at Trafalgar.

A pathos clings about Nelson then. He writes to Lady Hamilton indirectly, dwelling constantly on his interest in Mrs. Thomson, and her child. He calls himself " a friend of Mrs. Thomson," and says that he will " go mad with joy," that he " cries, prays, and performs all tricks." In the letter which he writes to Emma, vowing that he will resign his command, he calls Emma his own dear wife, and says, pathetic in his ignorance:

> " I never did love anyone else. I never had a pledge of love till you gave me one, and you, thank my God, never gave one to anybody else."

Indeed, men have given up career and life for women, but seldom more than Nelson could have done, sacrificing a reputation greater than any which Europe has known since. When Nelson is at sea always the thought of Lady Hamilton is with him. With rashness and with feeling he writes to her:

> " You, my own Emma, are my first and last thoughts, and to the last moment of my breath they will be occupied in leaving you independent of the world, and all I long in the world that you will be a kind and affectionate Mother to my dear daughter Horatia. But, my Emma, your Nelson is not the nearer being lost to you for taking care of you in case of events which are only known when they are to happen and to an all wise Providence. I hope for many years of comfort with you, only think of all you wish me to say, and you may be assured it exceeds if possible your wishes. May God protect

you and my dear Horatia prays ever your most faithful and affectionate."

Indeed, when he goes to victory and his death, he still cleaves to Emma. Here is a letter, and here a diary; both go far to prove the heroic character of the man. Here the note in the diary:

"Friday night at half-past ten, drove from dear, dear Merton, where I left all that I hold dear in this world, to go to serve my King and country. May the great God whom I adore enable me to fulfil the expectations of my country, and if it is His good pleasure that I should return, my thanks will never cease being offered up to the throne of His Mercy. If it is His good Providence to cut short my days upon earth, I bow with the greatest submission, relying that he will protect those so dear to me that I leave behind. His will be done. Amen. Amen. Amen."

And here the letter:

"My dearest beloved Emma, the dear friend of my bosom, the signal has been made that the enemies' combined fleet is coming out of port. May the God of Battles crown my endeavours with success; at all events I will take care that my name shall be always most dear to you and to Horatia, both of whom I love as much as my own life; and as my last writing before the battle will be to you, so I hope to God that I shall live to finish the letter after the battle. May Heaven bless you, prays your

"NELSON AND BRONTE."

He died in battle, and these were his last words: "Take care of my poor Lady Hamilton. Kiss me, Hardy. Remember that I leave Lady Hamilton and my daughter to my country."

She was alone. She was idle, extravagant, spoilt. She could not afford to live at Merton; creditors pursued her, and twice she was imprisoned for debt. She began to pester ministers to grant her money for services done to her country, to pester them in the name of Nelson. But all hated her, because she shed upon the great name no longer the lustre of the beauty she had afforded it when Nelson lived, but only the memory of shame. She was blackmailed, she was poor, she became unknown, she grew older. Without Nelson she was nothing, and at last, in poverty, she died at Calais at the age of fifty-two. Perhaps Nelson asked too much of a virtuous nation when the last breath that the hero drew framed these unheard words: "Remember that I leave Lady Hamilton and my daughter to my country."

BIBLIOGRAPHY

A Great Adventuress, by Joseph Turquan & Jules D'Auriac.

Nelson's Legacy, by Frank Danby.

The Hamilton and Nelson Papers, compiled by A. W. Thibaudeau.

Story of Lady Hamilton, by E. H. Moorhouse.

QUEEN VICTORIA

X. QUEEN VICTORIA

A WIFE

It is a curious feature that our estimates vary from century to century. Machiavelli, once looked upon as a model diplomat and servant of his king, is to-day considered to be a brilliant rogue. Cleopatra the siren is now rather Cleopatra the victim. Time levels reputations, and though by taking thought a man cannot add a cubit to his stature, yet he may do so by taking time.

The reputation of Queen Victoria has varied in this way, and rather swiftly. When in 1837 she came to the throne as a girl of eighteen, she was greeted joyfully because she was young, because her cheeks were rosy, and especially because she delivered the British people from a long line of kings, George III, George IV, William IV—all of them old, crusty, of none too good reputation. She relieved them also of the pretensions of the junior dukes, likewise old and unpopular. For some years she charmed. Then, after her marriage, as she fell under the influence of the entirely worthy, of the perhaps over-worthy prince consort, as she tried to maintain the autocratic tradition and kept upon politics a hand which the people thought too heavy, the Liberal elements of England came to resent her. Then, again, she received sympathy in her widowhood, and little by little gained the vast support of the respectable England of the eighteen-fifties, because she was a model queen and a model mother.

As she grew older she became a legend. Empress of India—this increased her legend. She became the idol of the army, which, as it liked to put it, "swung a sword for old Queen Vic." The toast "The Queen, God bless her," accompanied by the breaking of the glass in which the toast had been drunk, became a ritual in regimental messes, not only in England but in India, South Africa, Australia, wherever the Union Jack unfurled. And time increased the legend. As Queen Victoria achieved her fortieth, her fiftieth, her sixtieth year of reign, as she bridged the gap between the nineteenth and the twentieth centuries, she became an institution. She was important because she had always been, because she was older than almost any one of her subjects, because hardly any in the British Empire knew the sound of the word "king."

The Empire was attuned to a queen, to a feminine symbol which identified itself with the heraldic figure of Britannia. The people loved her because she represented the good old days, those days to which humanity always turns its eyes—forgetting the evil, remembering the good.

After her death there was a revulsion. She grew associated with the Victorian age, and most unjustly. The words Victorian Age are of course absurd, for they attach to Victoria a very great period, and activities of which she entirely disapproved. Even to-day many people connect in a muddled manner the reign of Victoria with the discoveries of Darwin—whom she looked upon as an infidel—with the developments in chemistry, the discovery of aniline dyes and coal-tar products, with the manufacture of steel, with telegraphy, railways, and the motor-car—in all of which she had no interest at all.

They even feel, since they cannot think it, that Queen Victoria is dimly connected with the verse of Browning and of Swinburne, when actually she was connected only with that of Tennyson. A period jewelled with literature, illumined by science, has been associated with a woman who spent one half of her life in dark widowhood.

But where Queen Victoria has suffered is in her association with another side of the Victorian period, its immense stuffiness, its passion for well-advertised religion and profitable philanthropy, its hideously strict morals combined with a universal looseness. She came to stand for hypocrisy, for the cant which is so often attributed to the British—and so the people began to laugh at her memory. Hence Mr. Lytton Strachey and his matchlessly clever but unmerciful work. Now again the pendulum begins to swing in the other direction. We see Queen Victoria as limited, but we begin to realise that much force of character and much generosity hides behind her prejudices, her regard for her dignity. And we even tell ourselves that to be a model wife and a model mother is, after all, not a disgrace.

The present chapter does not purport to relate the political history of Victoria, because hers is a troubled period involving domestic agitation and foreign war, spreading so far back that it touches the revolutionary agitation of the thirties, the granting of votes to nearly all men, war with Russia, the settlement of eastern Europe at Vienna in 1878, the mutiny of India against the British East India Company, and the annexation of India to the British realm, and lastly the South African War, which darkened the last days of the Queen.

It would be pointless to recite a history in which she took no definite part. Strive as she might to assert autocratic power, strive as Prince Albert might to take into his hands the reins of government, the Liberal movement of England was too strong; Queen Victoria could not actually affect affairs. She was in the hands of her Prime Ministers; Lord Melbourne made a friend of her and led her; Peel and Gladstone bullied her and led her; Disraeli flattered her and led her still more easily; Lord Salisbury acquired her confidence. But in one way or another the British Cabinet and the British Parliament remained supreme. Queen Victoria is not so much a great historical figure as a great historical symbol behind which, working with a needle and with an account-book, hides a very simple woman, a very good woman, who would have been quite as happy if fate had made her the wife of a comfortable merchant instead of queen of a realm spreading over five continents.

When Queen Victoria came to the throne at the age of eighteen, having been born in 1819, she was rather short, slightly inclined to plumpness, white-skinned, rosy-cheeked, and blue-eyed. She had pleasantly fair hair, and charming hands. She retained this appearance for many years; Winterhalter's picture of the royal family shows her much the same, rather full in the cheek, and, though too short, pleasantly proportioned. She had a natural grace of bearing, surprising since she was neither tall nor slim. She held her head in the way that novelists call queenly. She was not a woman with whom anyone could take a liberty. And yet she was very much an impulsive child. No doubt her education at the hands of her mother, the Duchess of Kent, had much to do with this. She had been brought up with the greatest simplicity and on the lines of a virtuous German girl. She had been taught the household crafts, taught to respect her mother, educated in French and in the gentler arts. She had been sent to bed early. She knew nothing of the world, having been brought up in royal seclusion to prepare her for her great part.

Thus her sudden royalty came upon her with no effect of shock. She did not feel unworthy of it, for she was conscious of her importance, and that at an early age. For instance, when she was six she reproached Lady Jane Ellice, who was playing with her toys, saying to her: "You must not touch these; they are mine; and I may call you Jane, but you may not call me Victoria."

She was prepared for her dignity, but she was not prepared for the difficult rôle which any constitutional queen must fulfil. If she had been an autocrat she would have found her part easier to play. She was intellectually fitted for the rôle, being well grounded in divinity, speaking English, French, German, Italian, some Latin, being interested in political economy, and in all that is serious. She preferred the instructive conversation of King Leopold of Belgium to that of more flighty courtiers. But though she had a good intellectual equipment, her temperament was such as to cause conflicts with her Ministers and with her people.

It is symbolic of her temperament that one of her first acts on becoming queen was to have her bed taken out of the room which until then she had shared with the Duchess of Kent. The latter was greatly surprised as she saw rising before her a queen who suddenly replaced the submissive daughter whom she had trained for eighteen years to respect and to obey her. Victoria wished to assert herself, and all through her life this remained a dominant motive. We shall see in her relations with Prince Albert how dominant it was.

She was also very obstinate, not obstinate in an evil and ugly way, but because she considered that she knew what was good for her country, and felt it her duty—her moral and religious duty—to insist that this course should be followed. For instance, her German blood, her German associations, always throughout her life inclined her to favour Germany and to oppose France, but she never submitted to the numerous attempts to influence her made by King Leopold and by German princelings—strive as they might to influence British policy, Queen Victoria followed no will except her own.

One manifestation of her obstinacy appeared when her first Prime Minister, the Whig Lord Melbourne, fell and was replaced by the Tory Sir Robert Peel. It is a well-established rule in the British system that the officials of the Court should change with the Government. It is not a foolish usage, since persons at the Court can substantially influence the decisions of the sovereign. Though the British constitution lays down that the sovereign must take the advice of his Ministers, there is no practical means of forcing the sovereign to place his signature at the foot of an Act of Parliament to which he may object. If the sovereign does refuse to sign an Act which Parliament insists upon, if a general election returns the same party to power, and if the sovereign again refuses to sign the Act, very serious consequences may follow. Revolution might follow.

This did not happen during the reign of Victoria. Her predecessor, William IV, did refuse to authorise the creation of new peers, which was necessary to force through the House of Lords the Reform Act of 1832, but when Earl Grey was again returned to power William IV submitted.

The object of this brief statement of British constitutional practice is as follows: while the sovereign cannot be coerced, the sovereign can be influenced; therefore it is not desirable that when one Government is in power the sovereign should be surrounded with its political opponents. Thus, when Lord Melbourne fell, the ladies of the bedchamber should have been replaced by ladies of another political complexion—appointed by Sir Robert Peel. The Queen objected. She had an affection for her ladies, and she defied Sir Robert Peel. She sought the support of Lord Melbourne; she took the opinion of the Duke of Wellington; both tried to reason with her, to make her realise her constitutional position, but she would not be moved. A political crisis followed, a crisis of such magnitude that Peel was unable to form a Government and that Lord Melbourne returned to power: a Minister resumed office because the young queen was strong enough to challenge a complete Cabinet supported by a Parliamentary majority.

This incident is not futile; it gives us the measure of Victoria and shows us that here was a personality capable of intense love, of intense hatred, and of endless determination to assert her rights.

Thus one year passed, then two, and it became essential that the Queen should marry, since otherwise the succession to the throne would revert to one of the surviving old and unpleasant dukes. The situation was peculiar, because Queen Victoria was essentially of her period, and therefore looked upon marriage as a young girl of that time should, namely as one of the cruel necessities which nature has laid upon mankind. She could not think of it, because such a preoccupation was unworthy of a young lady. In principle a marriage should have been arranged for her by her mother; she should have met the young man whom her mother chose, and she should have done her mother's will, not venturing to select her own husband, yet vowing to honour and obey him.

We see signs of this in her conversation. She tells Lord Melbourne that her feeling is quite against ever marrying. She describes the idea of marriage as odious; yet she keeps enshrined in her memory the thought of Albert. She had met the young prince at Coburg some years before; she had found him and his brother Ernest pleasant and good-looking boys, and she had treated them as playfellows. She did not forget Albert, and we find a reference in her diary which shows that three years before her marriage he had made upon her a strong impression. Yet she did not wish to marry, and one may suspect that she inherited the feeling that has dominated many British queens: Queen Elizabeth never married, but maintained favourites; Mary, Queen of Scots, married Darnley, but refused him the crown matrimonial. One may assume that Queen Victoria feared that in a husband she might find a master. She would not be a queen who had to do obeisance to a king.

But the necessities of the case and circumstances were against her. The circumstances were resented on one side by Lehzen, on the other by Stockmar. Fräulein Lehzen was the Queen's governess, and had remained with her, gaining influence—in fact, protecting her at times against the dominating desires of the Queen's mother. Being German, she feared for Victoria an alliance that might not be German. She knew that Victoria liked Albert; he was a typical and suitable German prince. The alliance would suit the aims of Lehzen. On the other side stood Stockmar, tutor to Prince Albert, who, little by little, had acquired power in the little Court of Coburg, and who for many years had conceived as a policy of State a marriage between Albert and Victoria. He had practically educated Albert to become the ruler of England.

Thus Victoria was hemmed in, and, though she showed aversion, the ground was not ill-prepared. Since she must marry, she might decide to look upon Albert without dislike. She summed up the matter of an interview with Albert as disagreeable, proclaimed that she would not look upon herself as bound, and ungraciously decided to receive at Windsor Albert and his brother Ernest. Five days later she knew herself to be in love.

The suddenness of this rush of emotion may be explained in various ways. It is possible that Victoria had long felt affection for Albert, and that she had concealed it, as was usual in those days; it is also conceivable that since she knew that a marriage between them was made desirable by reasons of family and of State, she was surprised to be attracted—convenience being seldom attractive—and thus went from relief to passion; it is also possible that, like any other human being, she fell in love at first sight.

Indeed the letter which she wrote to the King of the Belgians, immediately after the arrival of the princes, exhibits her interest. She says:

> "The dear cousins arrived at half-past seven on Thursday, after a very bad and almost dangerous passage, but looking both very well, and much improved. Having no clothes, they could not appear at dinner, but nevertheless *débutéd* after dinner in their *négligé*. Ernest is grown quite handsome; Albert's *beauty* is *most striking*, and he is so aimable and unaffected—in short, very *fascinating*; he is excessively admired here."

One perceived no intensity of feeling here; indeed the Queen goes on in the same letter to speak of certain lords, of political troubles in Spain, and she suggests in regard to the two princes only a pleasant visit in the country. It appears that she rides with them, that she dances with them, and that they play symphonies of Haydn. But Queen Victoria would have thought it undesirable to express too violently feelings that may already have been violent. Certainly she would have been cautious with the King of the Belgians, whose political patronage she already slightly resented.

But the Queen's letters and her diary almost at once reveal deeper feelings. She notices "the exquisite nose," "the delicate moustachios and slight but very slight whiskers," "the beautiful figure, broad in the shoulders and fine waist."

Indeed, Queen Victoria did not exaggerate. The portrait of Prince Albert by Partridge shows a rather broad, oval face with fine eyebrows, beautiful and abundant hair, slightly melancholy eyes, and a very delicate mouth. An expression of brooding sadness haunts the face without overwhelming it. It is an earnest face, such a face as might endow a successful actor, and therefore it is the face of the schoolgirl's dream. No wonder that Queen Victoria was attracted, for she was captured æsthetically, having reached the age of twenty without being impressed by men, save in their intellectual and moral attainments. Prince Albert had all the mental and moral qualities a woman might desire, and in addition he had beauty ; he could lay before her an attractive appearance and an irreproachable soul : thus she could indulge in her passion for him without feeling guilty.

Thus, five days after the arrival of Prince Albert at Windsor, Queen Victoria takes him aside, tells him, perhaps rather shyly, that he must be aware why she wished him and his brother to come to Windsor. Being Queen, she cannot accept addresses, but must pay them; she tells him that it will make her *too happy* if he will consent to marry her. The Queen then adds that they embraced, and that he was "so kind, so affectionate." Those words, "kind, affectionate," are slightly pathetic. The couple begins matrimony so—matrimonially. There glows in this passion no visible red light. It is a passion already domestic.

No doubt this was due to the fact that Prince Albert did not love Victoria. He liked her, he respected her, he had been taught by Stockmar that he was to marry her, and he realised that as Prince Consort he would have an opportunity to do good to a great people. But love had not entered into his mental composition, and it never so entered. He preferred the conversation of a geographer to that of any pretty lady; like a Puritan of the seventeenth century, he disliked humour, which he did not understand, and the light treatment of serious subjects. One may say that the Prince Consort never knew love. He was therefore in the best possible position for a husband—he could allow himself to be adored. And it is because he calmly—and kindly and affectionately—allowed Queen Victoria to throw her heart at his feet that after a few years he came to dominate the most imperious sovereign Great Britain had known since the death of Elizabeth.

Only a few months separated the engagement from the marriage, and those Queen Victoria passed in a

QUEEN VICTORIA AND PRINCE ALBERT

fever of anticipation. She was then like any ordinary girl fearing that fate might rob her of her happiness; she wrote every day to her future husband, while he prepared himself for the duties of marriage and of a great position. He rode, he stalked deer, he collected samples of animals and plants for his natural history collection, he played the piano, and he received the final instructions of Stockmar, determining to be indeed a father to his new people, to develop among them wealth, health, social service, to favour the opening of picture galleries, the printing of worthy books, and the pursuit of true religion. The Prince Consort is difficult to judge because a covert dullness hangs over the description of him which one is compelled to make, but again, as in the case of Victoria, let us record that there is nothing disgraceful in being a pious, hard-working, honourable, and well-meaning man. In days such as ours this observation is worthy of record.

At last the wedding-day came, and it did not come too soon. Victoria's temper, that had always been imperious, now became ungovernable. She was enervated because she feared that fate might disappoint her. She worked herself into a fever that compelled medical attention. Also, according to Mr. Lytton Strachey, she was terrified by the thought that now she came under an alien domination, that she must honour and obey Albert—she, Queen of England, obey. She vowed that she would never obey, that she would indeed stay queen, Albert she would love, honour, and—well, love and honour.

Indeed before the marriage the complications due to Queen Victoria's ardent temperament had already manifested themselves. She writes to Albert, who wished to choose his gentlemen:

"As to your wish about your gentlemen, my dear Albert, I must tell you quite honestly that it will not do. You may entirely rely upon me that the people who will be about you will be absolutely pleasant people, of high standing and good character. These gentlemen will not be in continual attendance on you; only on great occasions, and to accompany you when you go anywhere, and to dinners, etc. Seymour is your confidential attendant, and also Schenk and Anson, whom Lehzen has written to you about.

"Old Sir George Anson has been told of your gracious wish to have him as Groom of the Bedchamber and is delighted.

"*I* can only have *Lords*, and they will not be *Peers*, but *Lords*, the eldest sons of Dukes or Marquesses, or Earls (Counts), and who as far as possible are not in Parliament, for then they need not change, but your people are appointed by you and not by me (nominally) and therefore, unless you were to vote against my Government (which would be awkward), they need not change. You may rely upon my care that you shall have proper people, and not idle and not too young, and Lord Melbourne has already mentioned several to me who would be very suitable. . . ."

This confirmed the feeling of hesitation that Prince Albert may have experienced. He did not understand English politics well yet, and saw no more reason why he should not have about him the gentlemen he chose, and even gentlemen of his own nationality, than Queen Victoria, two years before, had seen why she should not have about her ladies of the bedchamber who suited her. But it never occurred to Queen Victoria that, while she might insist upon having her own ladies there was any reason why Prince Albert should have a right to his own gentlemen. Such was not her way of thinking. So Prince Albert received the gentlemen suitable for him, and was compelled to accept Lord Melbourne's former secretary. There exists no evidence that Albert actively resented the domination that was closing in about him. He may have expressed himself to Stockmar, but he was willing enough to accept that "uneasy lies the head that wears a crown," even a mere coronet.

Yet, since he could not respond to the bright, passionate feeling of Queen Victoria, he was at first not happy. London was not like Coburg ; the domestic virtues of his little duchy were not faithfully reproduced in England, still haunted by the excesses of the Georges ; the moral tone of England affronted his prejudices. He did not speak English well, and he had no habit of talking to women. Therefore he did not shine at Court, and he never to the end of his life understood the English political tradition which denied women all power of control, yet gave them so much power of intrigue. He was too grave ; he conversed too long with bishops, not long enough with butterflies. No doubt he would have become discontented, or might have devoted himself to some private hobby, if Stockmar had not insisted that he should avail himself of his influence over Victoria to take into his hands something of the control of the British Empire.

Stockmar, made a Baron, suffered from a peculiar kind of ambition. He desired no honours for himself, but he wished his pupil to dominate. So he stood behind Albert, persuading him that it was his duty to share control with the Queen and to take his part in British affairs. Thus began a struggle which lasted several years, a struggle of which very little appeared, because the Queen seldom refused an answer to Albert; she avoided him, she eluded him when he questioned her on a political matter; she referred him to smooth ministers, or she gave confused explanations. In fact, she was terrified; to her he was a man, to him she was a woman and a queen. Thus at first there was friction.

Queen Victoria liked to dance until morning, she enjoyed Court functions, she liked London—in other words, she was a worldling. Prince Albert liked to go to bed early, wished to surround himself with men of science and representatives of the arts. We do not know what happened in their domestic interior, but it is certain that they came now and then to the verge of quarrelling. If Prince Albert had not been a man of high character and great industry, he would have been worsted, but he set to work to become English, to learn English history, to gain an idea of English law; he made himself conversant with Parliamentary and constitutional practice.

Victoria did not notice what was going on, or at least decided that these studies were fitting to Albert's position. It was only by degrees, as his comments grew sound, as she was compelled to accept them, as she realised that Prince Albert had perhaps less character but more intellect than she, that unconsciously she allowed him to discuss politics with her and little by little to influence her. As Queen Victoria became more wholly wedded to him, he even managed to sever the old friendship which united his wife with Lord Melbourne. Then, perhaps because Stockmar was undermining her position, perhaps because the wish of Albert, now the father of her children, operated upon her, Queen Victoria found herself absorbed into the domestic relationship; thus she needed less Countess Lehzen, her governess and her old friend. Little by little Albert damaged Lehzen, and because he wished it Lehzen was sent away.

Within two years Victoria fell under the sway of Albert; within five she was his more than she was her own. Mr. Strachey draws a brief and amusing picture of their life. At Windsor they went for a walk before breakfast, while he told her which trees were which and educated her in the life of the bee. Or she would sit and do cross-stitch while he read aloud out of Hallam's *Constitutional History of England*. Or he would play the organ. Sometimes they played round games. Victoria's diary of that time is filled with rapturous descriptions of, and comments upon, Albert. She speaks of her real, solid happiness, which no reverses can damage: she thanks God that she now knows what is real happiness. She writes to King Leopold, crying out how blessed, how proud she is to possess so perfect a being. Meanwhile she falls completely under the sway of Albert, and admits him to work with her every day—in other words, to take a share with her in the government of the Empire.

Possibly he did not care for his life in England, and perhaps that was why he indulged in so many minor pleasures, but he did have a sacrificing passion: politics for the good of the people.

Prince Albert, well guided by Stockmar, did not advance too fast. His first reform was quite a mild one: he altered the arrangements of the household at Buckingham Palace, suppressed sinecures—kept down waste, brought order into the accounts—as if he were a thrifty housekeeper, as if Victoria had secured a good wife. But if she thought that, she was deceived, since she was dealing with Stockmar, one infinitely more subtle than herself. Stockmar understood, though he did not say so to Prince Albert, that, if a man controls the heart, he may begin by ruling the household and end by ruling an Empire.

And this happened. Albert became the confidential adviser of the Queen; his intercourse with Ministers increased, and these, who had begun by looking upon him as an intrusive German of rather dull mind, could not help recognising that always the Prince was sensible, always high-minded, that he never aspired to publicity—that he had honestly set himself as an object to help the Government without snatching the glory. Little by little the statesmen of the nineteenth century—Palmerston, Melbourne, and the others—were compelled to recognise an influence which grew. The Prince was not popular, but he was not unpopular. There were moments when his influence was believed to be pro-German, anti-Russian, or pro-French, when the English Liberal spirit revolted against his having any influence at all; but in the main he was looked upon as serious, and he was not detested.

Albert's influence was particularly strong in a direction where there could be no clash with Victoria. He was at heart a Tory, while Queen Victoria had been faithfully educated by Lord Melbourne as a moderate Whig, but was by temperament a benevolent autocrat, while Victoria was dominating and vain. Therefore he had no difficulty in persuading her that all public business was her business, that every measure must be submitted to her before it was put forward in Parliament, that every foreign dispatch must be read by her, approved by her, that foreign relations were her business. In other words, he lived mentally in the seventeenth century, when a royal marriage was more important than the decision of a Parliament, when nations went to war because two kings quarrelled, or because some noblemen commented disagreeably on the colour of the Queen's hair.

One can easily imagine how much this enhanced the passion of Victoria. Here was the man whom she had feared as a master working with her as a servant; here the person who was to contradict her, instead of fostering her self-esteem, strengthening her deepest prejudices. Thus child after child was born to them, thus they worked together, close companions as well as lovers, thus they were never apart, until Prince Albert became a necessity in her life, until he grew akin to the beat which governed it. She lived by him and for him. Though this love was moral, though it was domestic, though it resolved itself into stiff evenings by the fireside while Albert read from the *History of the Church of England*, it was love, true love, and the widowhood of Queen Victoria proves this better than any exclamations in the most passionate love-letter. She was not lyrical; she could not, exclaim: " Bring me upon thy heart and make me thine "; she could not say with Francis Thompson:

> And thou, what needest with thy tribe's black tents,
> That hast the red pavilion of my heart?

She could not leave us the outcry of a soul in rapture, for that was not the way in that time, but she could give herself entirely, live in constant worship before Albert's figure, and Albert's memory. She loved. Three years after her marriage she writes to the King of the Belgians, referring to the anniversary of her wedding as the dearest, happiest day in her life, to which she owes the present great domestic happiness she enjoys, which is greater than she deserves. Five years after her wedding she speaks of the life of constant self-denial which Albert leads, he who deserves every amusement in the world. She says that she is deeply touched by his accommodating spirit and his good-humour. After eight years of marriage she loves him still, says, " He is indeed looked up to and beloved, as I could wish he should be; and the more his rare qualities of heart and mind are known, the more he will be understood and appreciated."

When the end approaches she constantly writes to her uncle, the King of the Belgians, giving news of the invalid. He invades State correspondence. She could say of Albert what Shakespeare said of Cleopatra:

> Age cannot wither her, nor custom stale
> Her infinite variety—

that is, there was no variety in Albert, he was always the same, but always he poured out for Victoria the elixir of life.

Prince Albert died in 1861 at the age of forty-two, and his wife was to survive him forty-one years, forty-one years during which he lived by her side, during which she clove to him. She embraced his shadow with an intensity which could not have been paralleled about a quick body. Indeed it can be said that Queen Victoria died in 1861, that she was buried by Albert's side. For many years she lived entirely secluded, refusing to show herself to the people, until her ministers insisted that she should. She abandoned Court functions, of which she had been so fond. She forgot to smile, and she wore mourning until she died. The present writer remembers well his only glimpse of Queen Victoria in a State carriage in the early days of the South African War. In an open carriage came a very small old lady, under a close black bonnet, her head sunk into black material, her body shaped in thick black material without a glint. For a moment there was an effect of weariness, and she was gone.

Where the love of Queen Victoria exhibits itself completely is in the political course which she pursued after her husband's death. She set herself to execute the policy which by degrees he had endowed her with. Since Albert had laid down that she must know what the Cabinet did, so must she do. Because he wished her to read all dispatches, she must read all dispatches. Arduous as the work might be, wearisome as it must be, more and more concerned with subjects that did not interest her, she must do what Albert would have done. It is pathetic to think of this ageing woman, entirely divorced from modern feeling, unendowed by progress, striving to discover in compulsory education bills, in railway bills, in bills concerned with scientific and pedagogic training, with the admission of women to the local vote, the course which Albert would have followed. This love beyond the grave—this long, intellectual love—is indeed historic. In a sense it was perhaps morbid.

Indeed the word morbid is not too much, for Queen Victoria abandoned herself so entirely to the cult of the dead that she refused to recognise to herself that Albert was dead. At Windsor every night in the Prince's room, which was left as it was on the day of his death, an evening suit was laid on the bed, also clean linen, and hot shaving-water was placed in the beaker ready for the hand that would not move again. This is foolish, it is sentimental, but it has a grace. It is a sign that he was not forgotten, that Queen Victoria, by the light of her grief, was finding consolation. But she could not have found such consolation if she had not loved. If Prince Albert had been to her only a political mate, what would she have cared for the clothes into which he had imprinted his form?

In conclusion, because it contains so much of her feeling for him, its modesty, its gentleness, its commonplace and yet delicate nature, one may reproduce the love-letter which Queen Victoria wrote to Albert on their wedding morning:

> "DEAREST— . . . How are you to-day, and have you slept well? I have rested very well, and feel very comfortable to-day. What weather! I believe, however, the rain will cease.
>
> "Send one word when you, my most dearly loved bridegroom, will be ready.
>
> "Thy ever-faithful,
>
> "VICTORIA R."

BIBLIOGRAPHY

Readers interested in this character will find further information in the following works:

The Letters of Queen Victoria, edited by A. C. Benson and Viscount Esher (3 vols.).

Queen Victoria, a biography, by Sidney Lee.

Queen Victoria, by Lytton Strachey.

Leaves from the Journal of our Life in the Highlands, 1848 to 1861, edited by A. Helps.

More Leaves from the Journal of our Life in the Highlands.

The Early Court of Queen Victoria, by Clare Jerrold.

The Married Life of Queen Victoria, by Clare Jerrold.

The Widowhood of Queen Victoria, by Clare Jerrold.

Victoria, Queen and Ruler, by E. Crawford.

The Life of Queen Victoria, reproduced from *The Times*, 1901.